PRAISE FOR *A HOLE IN THE CLOUDS*

"I was pretty independent most of my life. I had flight guidebooks and would select my own flights. But Casto Travel always did an excellent job of finding hotels and suggesting trips. Eventually, Casto could do a better flight-booking job with their computers than I could do myself, so I used Casto exclusively for any important travel for a decade or two in my life. Casto is the only travel agency that I remember. I struggle to find the personal attention I received from Casto Travel in every aspect of my life these days. *A Hole in the Clouds* explains how and why they treated me so well."

> —Steve Wozniak, Apple cofounder, designer, and engineer

"Poignant, touching and insightful, I enjoyed reading *A Hole in the Clouds* so much. Maryles is brilliant—a legend, a class act, and an inspiration to women, mothers, entrepreneurs, and humanity in general."

> —Charlene Leiss, president, Flight Centre
> Travel Group, The Americas

"Those of us who know and travel with Maryles are witness to all she has built; the lives she has touched; the rich legacy of stories from her childhood; her growth of the business among Silicon Valley legends; her loves and losses, family, and so many friendships. *A Hole in the Clouds* is the American dream of a young immigrant woman who built a thriving business from the ground up because her eyes saw only the blue sky beyond the clouds, and her heart told her nothing was impossible.

"Her business was built on love . . . love of travel, flying, hospitality, and most importantly—family. Her clients, vendors, employees, and all of us lucky enough to be friends with this fearless, charming, and inspiring entrepreneur feel we, too, are family.

"Maryles's life and this book are a master class in what it takes to be a successful entrepreneur."

—Mary Huss, market president and publisher, *San Francisco Business Times* and *Silicon Valley Business Journal*

"WOW. *A Hole in the Clouds* is a page-turner. So many of us raised kids, managed our careers, and can identify with many aspects of this story. Bravo to you, Maryles. I hope our daughters read this. It is inspiring."

—Mary M. Bersot CFA, Bersot Capital Management LLC

"I can honestly say that Casto Travel was an integral part of our success. Without the efficient and accurate travel plans Conner Peripherals would never been able to keep up with the growth for those ten years. Flights, hotels, and all other travel needs were handled with total professionalism. My thanks to Maryles and her team for their support. *A Hole in the Clouds* is a blueprint for how to build a truly customer-first service business."

—Finis Conner, cofounder of Fortune 500 companies Seagate Technology and Conner Peripherals

"Maryles Casto is an inspiration for all of us. Her obsession with excellent customer service combined with her gutsy risk-taking determination produced a remarkable entrepreneur. Her immigrant story, told in *A Hole in the Clouds*, is about landing in Silicon Valley, but her success is all about seizing its opportunities."

—Connie Martinez, Chief Executive Officer, SVCREATES

"This is the American story of one immigrant woman's success that is a model for us all: unflagging efforts to succeed, personal confidence, and perseverance over time. This is a book for anyone who sustains the American dream."

—Judy Koch, former owner of RSP Manufacturing Corporation, founder of the Bring Me a Book foundation, and C200 member

"Maryles not only lives the American dream . . . she is the quintessential entrepreneur! Her passion and energy are intoxicating! Bravo!"
—Josie Cruz Natori, CEO and founder of the Natori Company

"It's early days in Silicon Valley—a wildfire of technological innovation—the doers being mostly white and all male. Into this forbidding neighborhood walks a young Filipina who wants to start a nontech business. *A Hole in the Clouds* is a tale of a pubescent Silicon Valley and someone who, although checking none of the right boxes, prevails. Maryles has a great story to tell."
—Irwin Federman, USVP

"In today's fast-changing world where social inequity, technology acceleration, and disruptive business models place a premium on purpose-driven leadership, Maryles Casto's journey and insights provide a case study in courage, compassion, and principle-based decision-making. It is a must-read for anyone seeking inspiration and insights for navigating uncertainty, adversity, and the continuous pursuit of the next horizon."
—Brad D. Smith, executive chairman, Intuit

"Maryles Casto's amazing immigrant-to-multimillion-dollar-businesswoman success story is an inspiration not only to all immigrants who have to work harder for equal space in the corporate world, but also to women who strive within an environment mostly occupied by men. She exemplifies what Filipino hospitality is all about with her clients by making them feel at home and part of the Casto Travel family. This is the secret to her success."
—Mona Lisa Yuchengco, publisher, PositivelyFilipino.com

"I have known Maryles for many, many years and have watched her creative business acumen revolutionize the travel agencies as they have been operated. Her commitment to her employees and customers is unparalleled."
—George Marcus, chairman of Marcus & Millichap and Essex Property Trust

"Maryles is an inspiration and role model. She is an entrepreneur in the truest sense, having created and re-created herself many times. *A Hole in the Clouds* can teach us all how to dream bigger, believe in ourselves, and never take *no* for an answer. She is a true pioneer of the Silicon Valley."

—Naomi Kelman, CEO Willow Innovations, Inc.

"Maryles Casto is an important community leader in Silicon Valley, San Francisco, California, and the Philippines. She is also a wonderful storyteller, and she has drawn on her personal, business, and public life to write a fascinating tale!"

—Dr. Gloria C. Duffy, president and CEO, The Commonwealth Club

A Hole
in the
Clouds

A HOLE IN THE CLOUDS

FROM FLIGHT ATTENDANT TO SILICON VALLEY CEO

MARYLES CASTO

SILICON
VALLEY
PRESS

Published by Silicon Valley Press, Carmel, CA
Siliconvalleypress.net

Design: Paul Barrett
Image credits: Cover © 2021/1980 George Wedding/GEOPIX. Interior images
from Maryles Casto's personal collection

ISBN (hardcover): 978-1-7358731-5-2
ISBN (e-book): 978-1-7358731-6-9

Lovingly for Marc, Elenora, and Abigail

*And know that yesterday is but today's
memory and tomorrow is today's dream.*

*But if in your thoughts you must measure time into
seasons, let each season encircle all the other seasons,*

*And let today embrace the past with
remembrance and the future with longing.*

—From *The Prophet* by Khalil Gibran

CONTENTS

FOREWORD

Each of us carries upon our history the interaction of all the people we have met and engaged with in some way great or small. They are our close intimates, from family to dearest friends; others are the myriad strangers engaged briefly when purchasing coffee, sharing the same subway, or presenting our boarding pass while stepping onto one more flight. At times, though, the great divide of human connection is surpassed, and a stranger becomes a friend.

Too many of us have a deep fear of the stranger, of their thoughts and impressions; for Maryles, someone she has yet to meet is a story still to be learned. At a charity cocktail reception, a July Fourth barbecue, or a formal state dinner, Maryles is at ease and comfortable, eager to introduce like-minded people or otherwise make connections where none yet exist.

I vividly recall one evening at Santa Clara University, at an event hosted by the Commonwealth Club of California. The keynote speakers were two young tech savants with a novel product, a recent round of capital raised, and a notion that would either take the Valley by storm or fizzle like a firework left out during the spring rains. Seizing the opportunity, Maryles led the two of us forward through the sea of onlookers and introduced herself with, "Hi, I'm Maryles Casto. I'm your travel agent. So, what is a search engine? Is it really important?" Sergey Brin stared at her, briefly mystified, then, with a large smile, he spent the next ten to fifteen minutes explaining the intricacies of the internet . . . and why it would put her out of business. This was more than twenty years ago, and as you will discover, his predictions proved untrue.

Another event had her sitting at a table as former 49ers coach Bill Walsh explained the complexities of the West Coast offense. One more witnessed the culmination of an event she'd planned for months, uniting a number of local notables to meet with Queen Noor of Jordan and review opportunities to encourage female entrepreneurship in the Middle East. Many more such stories exist, some of which you will read about here.

This is not to say Maryles is a collector of celebrity encounters; this truly could not be further from the truth. She has no interest in celebrity, pomp, or pretense. Gossip, intrigue, drama, and ceremony bore her mightily. Of interest to her are people and their stories, what makes them genuine.

Her own story is fundamentally the one of Silicon Valley: an immigrant with passion, determination, and a profound desire to innovate building a new path and a new life for herself. While her skills were not to be found in coding, engineering, or investing, they were just as critical: the art of making a human connection. In this book, you will also find her lessons for success that every entrepreneur, or student of the Valley, would do well to heed.

If you ask Maryles, she will likely say that Casto Travel gave her the ability to make these connections throughout business and life. The truth of the matter is that her ability to connect enabled Casto Travel to succeed where many before failed and that Casto Travel is truly a product of her compassion and profound interest in the fortune of others.

One practice that she carries to this day is writing a personal letter on each birthday and anniversary for every single employee, all in her signature print and penmanship—never a form letter and always an honest expression of appreciation for the individual, complete with personal details about family, events, windfalls, and pitfalls pertinent to the person. Many people at Casto Travel had ten, twenty, or even thirty years with the firm. Nearly all retained each and every letter they received.

Not that it comes easy. As you will see in her story, she provides an honest and intimate reflection on her challenges, successes, and failures. At times, her business succeeded wildly; at other times, it teetered on the edge of bankruptcy. With it came the emotional toil and strain of carrying and caring for the well-being of others. In some cases, the pain is still real and raw, and while she does not show it upon her face, it rests upon her soul.

As you will learn, the title of this book is a reference to a flying lesson her own father shared with her, one that she draws upon to this day. The relevance of the lesson is in no small measure due to her own love of flying.

Many years ago, I received a call from her, saying, "You'll never guess what I just did."

"Okay, what did you do?" I asked.

"I flew an F-16."

With astonishment, I responded, "An F-16? The military plane? With missiles and all that?"

"Yes," she responded with glee, "the real thing. No missiles, though."

She then recounted how she was invited to participate in an event sponsored by the US Department of Defense. At its conclusion, they offered up the chance to ride in an F-16 to two of the members of the committee. Not surprising anyone, she immediately volunteered.

Donning the full suit and helmet, she entered the plane with her pilot ("He was really cute!"), went through the preflight checklist, hit the afterburners, and pierced the sky. After a series of aggressive maneuvers, likely designed to test her fortitude, the plane hit cruising altitude and the pilot released the controls to her.

"I felt free. So very free. God, we were going fast!" For the next thirty minutes or so, she lived a dream.

Mind you, the other volunteer did not fare as well. That plane had to make an emergency landing due to his inability to keep his lunch down. There may have been a smirk of pride on her face as she retold the story.

Few have the gift to connect with everyone they meet as does Maryles Casto. Time and again, in cities near and countries far, I have heard people say, "Please give your mother my regards. She is truly a wonderful person. There is something honestly amazing about her. I really feel we connected."

As her son, I am honored to respond, "You did. You really did connect with her. And she is something."

Marc Casto, President, Leisure Americas, Flight Centre Travel Group

PREFACE

The word *entrepreneur* was first used to describe me by a business friend on a trip to Alaska we took forty-five years ago. Not understanding what it meant, I was not sure if she had insulted or complimented me. I chose the latter.

If my risk-taking instincts, independence, competitiveness, passion to love completely, ability to see no hurdles to overcome, and capacity to manage the conflicts and demands of family and career make me an entrepreneur, then yes, I accept that compliment.

The story I tell here is how I, as an immigrant, found a new home in America, lived as a woman pioneer in this place called Silicon Valley, and navigated the adventures, romance, and surprises that befell me along the way. I was constantly learning and growing and have included my own lessons learned that will hopefully be helpful to others.

I have made an effort to recall and write an honest personal version of my mistakes and vulnerabilities, some painful to remember. I wrote this book because it was time to do so. This story is a genuine portrait of what women were experiencing in the early '60s, as it related to me. I needed to bring my story to a much larger audience so it can be heard. It is a story about a Filipina immigrant choosing this country to call home, a daughter whose father taught her to dream and look for her hole in the clouds—encouraging fathers to do the same for their daughters. A story about a career- and businesswoman, providing a good example to the students who will be tomorrow's leaders. A story about family, sharing experiences with the mothers and grandmothers who are rejoicing being part of their loved ones' yesterdays, todays, and tomorrows. Most of all, a story about the privilege of being a part of the Casto world, so readers can experience what I have experienced, learn what I have learned, and love as I have loved. I am grateful to all of you who shared my voyage and kept the lights burning. I am the fortunate one, having you all be my inspiration.

INTRODUCTION

SPOTLIGHT

"Are you ready for this?"

My brother Gus and I stood on the steps in front of the double doors of Harvard Business School. It was 1997. We had flown from San Francisco to Boston the night before, checked in at a nearby hotel, eaten a desultory dinner. After a morning devoted to our separate projects, we had reunited here, in front of the great redbrick and white-wood Colonial-style building, with its four-columned portico and distinctive cupola rising far above us.

Am I ready?

Gus's question transported me back to our flight to Boston. Buckled into my seat, I had watched the flight attendants move back and forth between the galley and their passengers, pouring drinks, delivering meals, handing out blankets. *That was me,* I thought. At eighteen years old, during the golden age of airline travel, I became a stewardess, as we were called then, for Philippine Airlines. Suddenly I could see my past as if I were watching a movie: tucked into my smart uniform, commanding the galley, striding the aisles, anticipating each of my passenger's needs. Now I was in the passenger seat, a Silicon Valley entrepreneur, founder of a global travel company, invited to Harvard Business School, where Casto Travel would be presented as a case study. It was a surreal moment—as if I had blinked and become the person I am today.

Silicon Valley woman takes on Harvard.

As I stood on the threshold of the business school, my brother's question hanging in the air, I took in our surroundings, and it hit me again: we were a long way from the plantation where we grew up in the Philippines, even from the shiny new buildings of Silicon Valley. *What am I doing here?*

I had never attended a day of college, much less business school. I was always too restless in a classroom. I was a farm girl, after all, and compared to the days I spent outdoors, running free with my siblings and the children of the people who worked on our property, school felt like prison.

Raised in a privileged family, I was destined—according to my parents—to marry into a family like mine and take my place in society, but I had different plans. I pursued the only career option available to young women in the Philippines in 1959. Later, as a newlywed immigrant in the United States, to make ends meet, I sold Avon products door-to-door and wrapped gifts at Macy's. Eventually, I returned to my first love, travel. I learned the travel agency business by working for others, then put my own stake in the ground, building what would become Silicon Valley's go-to travel agency, growing up alongside the tech giants who were creating the digital world we live in now.

But in 1997, business experts were predicting that travel agencies were doomed, soon-to-be victims of the new e-commerce trend, which would enable travelers to purchase their own airline tickets and make their own hotel reservations over the internet. So here I was, at one of the most renowned business schools on Earth, about to speak to a room filled with the best and brightest business minds in the United States about my supposedly crumbling industry.

The young men—and they would *all* be men—in that classroom had studied the growing virtualization of America's travel industry. They had been briefed on Casto Travel's history. They had been posed three questions: What should Maryles Casto do to counter these dramatic shifts in her business? Has the business model shifted to such an extent that she should leave the business? What advice do you have for Casto and her executive team?

But those young men didn't know anything about the woman who was about to walk into their lives.

"I'm ready," I told Gus. In saying so, I realized it was true. Surprisingly, I felt calm and assured.

First of all, I was an emissary from the real world, the ever-evolving, wildly competitive territory of Silicon Valley, and I was there to tell those students of theory how things actually worked on the ground, in day-to-day business. More importantly, I knew I had the key to this emerging threat to the travel industry called "the internet," and no one, not even a bunch of brilliant B-school neophytes, was going to talk me out of it.

Gus and I looked at each other, nodded in agreement, and walked through the double doors into an alien world.

Minutes later, I found myself in a lecture hall facing a middle-aged professor and fifty young men, all of them looking at me as if I had just arrived from Mars. Not only was I a woman executive—a rare species in the late twentieth century—but I didn't look like the stereotypical businesswoman. As a child, I had always worn custom-made dresses, which had given me a taste for elegant clothing that never left me. So, the last thing I was going to wear standing before the class that day was a dark suit with a big pale bow. No, I was wearing Adam Beall, a designer in whom I had invested, a dress that would have been appropriate for a museum opening. I was ready for the spotlight.

Being from Silicon Valley did not help my credibility in the eyes of these students. From their seats on the East Coast, in those early internet days, the tech industry still looked like a flash in the pan somewhere out in the Wild West, run by weird eccentrics and arrogant nerds. These young men were almost universally preparing for traditional careers in banking and finance—none of that California wildcatting for them.

When the professor introduced me as Maryles Casto, founder and CEO of Casto Travel, I could see the skeptical, bemused looks on the students' faces. To them, I was little more than a novelty, a proud little woman with an accent whom they would play with for an hour, then destroy. *I'll show them,* I told myself.

As Gus settled into a seat in the back of the room and I took my place up front, the professor asked the class to give a show of hands: "How many of you believe travel agencies will be gone in ten years?"

Forty-nine hands went up. Only one believed my company would survive. Now I understood what I was up against. In looking at me, these young men were not only seeing a novelty but the walking dead—a person who was so naïve that she remained optimistic even as her world was collapsing around her.

But I was not deterred. Casto Travel, and I, would survive, even if the rest of my industry evaporated.

Why was I so confident? Part of it was my personality: I have always been ferociously competitive. I hate to lose even more than I like to win, and I will fight to the death not to fail. In that way, as I discovered very quickly after my arrival in Silicon Valley, I have much more in common with the high-tech entrepreneurs I worked with than with the traditional travel agents I met. There was a fire in me—and in my Valley neighbors—that I did not see in that classroom.

But more than that, I had the confidence of a person with a survival strategy, one I had tested with my clients, one I knew how to execute. Unlike my audience, whose confidence was derived by their academic successes, the jobs that were awaiting them, and their abilities to dissect case studies, my confidence was forged in the crucible of a famously fast-moving, innovative, and competitive business region.

In one respect, those students and their professor were right: the internet was going to crush the traditional travel agency. But in serving the likes of Intel, Apple, Cisco, Sun, Juniper Networks, and others—that is, in serving the people building the internet's processors, servers, networks, platforms, and content—I had already identified the virtual revolution that was about to happen, and I was already constructing a fundamentally new model for a travel agency that would take advantage of this transformation. That's why I didn't just believe that I was right; I knew it.

My only task now was to show them why Casto Travel would not only survive but thrive.

For the next hour, I did just that. My presentation revolved around the story of a single company, which happened to be one of the hottest in the world at that moment: Silicon Graphics, Inc.

SGI had scheduled an international meeting of its senior management in Munich, Germany. At that moment, the company was flying so high that it offered all of its executives and their spouses an all-expenses-paid trip to the meeting and a host of other tours and activities. With all of those travelers, plus all of those events and side trips—not to mention any journeys the travelers wanted to make before and after the meeting—the travel arrangements promised to be a logistical nightmare.

Using a traditional travel agency model, I would have to hire a small army of temps to accommodate all the trip permutations and special requests. Even so, providing each traveler with our signature Casto Travel level of service would be nearly impossible. I had spent years building up goodwill in the Valley, and the last thing I wanted was to disappoint such an influential client.

That's when I had an epiphany: Why not do what all of my clients were doing with their businesses? That is, migrating traditional activities to the web, using the scalability potential of cyberspace, and enlisting the customers themselves into creating their own solutions? We did just that: we built our own webpage and then enabled all of those SGI execs and their spouses to link into that page and design their own itineraries. Then we took those itineraries and made them reality.

Today, that solution is so common that it seems obvious. But in the mid-nineties, it was a revelation. No one had attempted to virtualize the travel reservation process using the web. Better yet, the strategy worked even beyond my expectations: we were able to accomplish with a half dozen employees what I had estimated would have taken as many as thirty agents using the traditional process. Moreover, because each traveler had intimate control over their individual travel agendas, the SGI execs were more satisfied with the experience than ever before.

That's what I explained to the Harvard Business School class. Sure, it had taken a year's worth of planning, reorganizing, and re-equipping the agency to prepare the Casto team to operate smoothly in cyberspace, but it worked. Because we had learned not to fear the internet but to embrace it.

I absorbed this attitude from the best business teachers I could have asked for: men and women who were building the businesses of the future, like Bob Noyce, Andy Grove, and Steve Jobs—individuals who today are recognized as the greatest business executives of their age. Working with these men and women, famous and uncelebrated, had given me a perspective on both technological innovation and business strategy that I could never have learned in a classroom. Many are gone now, but they changed the world before they left, and I was blessed that they mentored me.

Sure, those students had crunched the numbers on the travel industry and concluded most travel agencies were doomed—and they were right about that. But by the end of my presentation, they understood that Casto Travel wasn't a traditional agency. We were not going to adapt to change; we were going to drive it. We would lead the way into this new world.

Did I convince them? I didn't need to—the impending dot-com explosion would do that. But what I did want to do was show them that they didn't know everything about the changing business world. They needed to rethink both their assumptions and their conclusions. Most of all, for all of the reasons they had dismissed me—a stylishly dressed woman with an accent, a travel agent from the Philippines by way of Silicon Valley—I was a force to be reckoned with, and they should listen to what I had to say.

In that, I succeeded. After my presentation, a number of the students came to the front of the room to talk to me. Some asked me about my background, others about what it was like to live in Silicon Valley. Still others asked me how we had come up with the new business model and its supporting software. One even asked if I could book a European trip for him.

As my brother rejoined me and we walked out of the classroom, that surreal feeling returned: I had done it. A self-taught businessperson, I had walked into Harvard Business School, into a room full of theorists convinced of my failure, and I had shown them exactly how Casto Travel would succeed.

Suddenly I was so tired that I could barely share my victory with Gus—exhausted and exhilarated, as if I had walked every step of my journey from the airplane galley to the upper echelons of Silicon Valley in one day.

On our flight home, Gus would tell me that he never doubted I would triumph at Harvard. All I had known was that I was not going to fail—at Harvard, or with Casto Travel, though many challenges awaited me back home.

MY PURPOSE

In the pages that follow, I propose to give a similar presentation to that one I gave that day a quarter century ago. But this time, the topic is my life and career—and the turning points that have decided my failures and successes. Along the way, I will reintroduce you to a number of now-legendary figures in business—not as they appear in their official biographies but as I knew them, as real flesh-and-blood individuals, with their genius, their eccentricities, and their foibles, when they triumphed and when they were filled with doubt. Some of these stories may make historians and biographers rethink their opinions and conclusions.

But more importantly, it is my hope that anyone who dreams of breaking the mold the world has cast for them, anyone who imagines taking the entrepreneurial leap, will find in these pages the message that no matter where you begin and no matter the naysayers you meet along the way, with enough ambition, courage, hard work, and—most of all—commitment to others, you can realize your dreams. You can stand confidently before even the most skeptical critics, and in some way small or large, you can change the world.

CHAPTER 1

FATHER AND DAUGHTER

I am my father's daughter.

My mother was raised in a world of elegance in the Philippines. It is telling that her privileged upbringing did not make her cold to those less well-off, but even more empathetic. Her name, Caridad, means charity—a word she embodied. She was a gentle and deeply religious woman who dedicated much of her life to her children, to the church, and to doing good works. She expressed a childlike delight in the beauties of the world, from art to music to the wonders of nature, and she played the piano beautifully. To this day, my siblings and I cannot hear the song "Autumn Leaves" without thinking of her fingers on the keys. But my mother's kindness is what I remember most about her. It is her voice that reminds me always to treat clients and employees well. My sense of duty and charity comes from my mother, but in so many ways, I am much more like my father.

Rafael Vallejo—my father—worked his way to success. Though he was born in the Philippines, his upbringing reflected his parents' Spanish background. Even as he became ever more deeply involved in Philippine life, he kept that heritage alive. He was a man small in stature but large in impact—always proud and immaculately dressed, with fierce eyes that belied a big heart. He conveyed so much with those eyes that he didn't need to talk much. The eyes did the job: with our household staff, employees on our farms, and even his children.

He was an orderly, disciplined man, and the role he took on as the head of our sugar plantation spilled over into our homelife. Dinners were serious affairs where we children, if we wanted to speak, had to come prepared. If the chatter among us slipped into slang or the local dialect, my father would glare and announce, "Spanish." From that moment on, Spanish was the language of the table, which we hated, so we usually lapsed into sullen silence. After dinner, the entire family would go out on the balcony to play dominoes, a game I still play to relax. The game wasn't about relaxation for my father, though—it was an opportunity to teach strategy. No matter how hard we tried, he could see what we were going to do five steps before we did it.

But there was another side to my father, one he invited me to see.

He was a pilot, and he owned his own plane, which he used to fly between the family's different farms—a much more efficient way to travel than on difficult roads, often through the jungle. When he would return from one of his business trips, he would always make one low pass by the house before touching down on the landing strip. That was a signal for all of us to race out to the runway to meet him as he taxied up.

My brothers and sisters varied from moderate to zero interest in flying, but I was obsessed with it. Flying just seemed so exciting and liberating. Secretly, I wanted to be a bird. Not to mention flying was so much a part of my father's personality—a side of him I longed to know. For his part, he seemed to understand that, of his seven children, I was the one most like him. So, while the engine was still warmed up, he would take me for a flight.

These weren't long flights, but my father always made them exciting. My job was to, in his words, "look for a hole in the clouds," which we could climb through into the clear blue above, where the air was perfect and the flying smooth, where he could perform simple acrobatic maneuvers that thrilled me every time. Up there, the mask of the tough-minded businessman, the strict disciplinarian, fell away. We were off on a shared adventure, our conversations freed from the formalities of life on the ground. Looking back, this was the beginning of my lifelong love of flying—an infatuation that has defined my career.

The father I got to know during those flights rarely made an appearance on the ground, but I did see him emerge in Spain once. Immersed in the Spanish culture, he was a different man: relaxed, charming, social—I even watched, with amazement, as he danced up a storm. By then, I was old enough to realize that the stern father of the plantation was a persona my father had adopted to succeed in a tough business on the other side of the world. His efforts to recreate Spanish life and culture in the Philippines—demanding we speak his native tongue at the dinner table—were his overly serious attempts to share with us a heritage he loved. The Philippines had made him a successful businessman, but his heart was Spanish.

My mother understood that; I think it was one of the things that she loved about him.

As for us kids, we were a pretty normal lot—three girls and four boys, entangled in all the usual teasing, bickering, and scheming. Our earliest years we spent playing together in the wide-open spaces of the plantation and our family home, but when we reached school age, one by one, we were sent off to boarding schools, boys to one and girls to another. From that point on, we came back together only in the summer and on school holidays. When we were reunited, we spent all our time together. We loved each other deeply, and that feeling only grew over the time we spent apart.

By birth order, I was a middle child, but in many ways, I was always the outlier of our pack, not just because my interests were different, but in inexplicable ways, I was just wired differently. I didn't like to sit still. I was always looking for the next big adventure, dreaming up my next big idea. In hindsight, I think it was my entrepreneurial personality making an early appearance.

My father saw that difference. He understood me in ways that neither my siblings nor my mother ever really did. As a result, he always paid special attention to me. No matter what plan I concocted or potential I showed, he responded with great patience as I developed it. He was not a naturally patient man—like me, he was a doer. Yet, I remember that as a young girl I decided that I was going to grow up and become a hairdresser—and I decided I needed to get an early start by working on my father's hair. So, this powerful, busy man would sit before me and let me work on his hair, combing it this way and that endlessly. It must have killed him to sit there like that, but he always let me go on as long as I wanted.

Recognizing that I was not cut out for a life typical of my peers—boarding school, then finishing school, then marriage into a Filipino family with standing—my father continued monitoring my development as I cut my own path, even into adulthood. I cannot emphasize enough how important that was to me: The life of an outlier can be very lonely, filled with more struggles and failures than joys and successes. But knowing that my father was there for me, supporting me when I took risks, warning me when he feared I would go off track, celebrating my wins—that was both an enormous comfort and a source of strength as I grew my wings and learned to fly on my own.

DIVIDED EXISTENCE

Throughout my education, I had two lives: one at home, where I was mostly happy, and one at school, where I usually was not.

With my family, I lived in a large home surrounded by lush gardens and mango trees I loved to climb—no better place to read a book than in the embrace of those branches. Balconies wrapped the exterior of the house, and wide steps led to the entrance. Inside, a beautiful foyer entered into a hallway stretching in each direction to our separate bedrooms. At one end of this hallway hung a grand painting of my Swiss grandfather, my mother's father, who had first built the plantation. He had white hair and piercing blue eyes. Across from him was my Filipina grandmother, with her flowing brown hair and brown eyes. The contrast between the two cultures was striking.

My grandfather had come to the Philippines from Switzerland at age eighteen, leaving behind his childhood girlfriend to seek his fortune on the other side of the world. There he met the Filipina daughter of one of his workers, who according to tradition paid a tribute to the "Patron" by serenading him, and he fell in love and married her. But not long after bearing him seven children, my mother being the youngest, my grandmother died in an accident. My grandfather, now a widower, went back to Switzerland and reconnected with his old girlfriend, who had since married, had seven kids, and had herself been widowed.

They married, and my grandfather brought her and her children to the Philippines, where his new wife raised my mother. Her large portrait hung at the other end of this hallway, and those three figures watched over all of us—my parents, us children, and the household staff—as we hustled past during the day.

The plantation itself was one thousand acres planted in sugarcane, and we had a second plantation in the mountains that grew coconuts. It was a remarkable life—though, at that age, I hardly noticed. My world was playing freely with my siblings and the children of the people who worked on the farm—fishing, riding water buffalos, and exploring this little island in the water out in front of the property. Years later, in America, trying to make a living selling Avon products door-to-door, I sometimes thought back on those days and they seemed like a dream—like someone else's life.

By comparison, the girls' Catholic boarding school my sisters and I attended was a nightmare. There I experienced a minute-by-minute regimentation so utterly different from my life at the plantation that I didn't know what to do with it. Unlike my mother and the women who helped take care of us at home, the nuns who ran the school were impossibly strict and deeply impatient. Not to mention that my family—which, to me, included the household staff, the people who worked on the farm, and their kids—had always been my closest friends. Now I was separated from them. Socially, I did well with my classmates, but with the nuns? Well, combine my free-range lifestyle at home with my increasingly maverick personality—I'm just not good at rules and regulations—and I became an eternal discipline problem.

Worse, I was an indifferent, distracted student. When a teacher would say, "First you do step one, then step two, then step three . . . ," my attitude was always, "Why can't we just jump to step ten and get it done?" I quickly lost interest in the lesson, the teachers lost patience with me, and I went from being bored to outright naughty in seconds. I'd hide so the nuns would have to take time to find me. I'd make fun of their huge, starched white wimples. My pranks stretched beyond the classroom, too. Because I hated going to confession, I'd do things like put on fake glasses and pretend to be someone else to confuse the priest. I was a terror, and none of their disciplinary measures could stop me.

It came to a head one day when I was particularly naughty in class—who knows what I did, but I'm sure it was awful. The sister teaching the class couldn't handle me, so she called the principal. When she arrived, she was furious with this troublesome child and decided to take extra measures. First, I was ordered out of the classroom. Then, the principal decided my punishment: she put a wastebasket over my head and ordered me to walk through every classroom in the school to put my shame on display before the entire student body.

If it was meant to humiliate and silence me, the punishment backfired. I decided to turn it to my advantage. So, when I arrived at each room, I would start dancing down the aisles, or singing, or doing anything else I could think of to bring the fun. At one point, I even stuck flowers into the wastebasket. Anything to get attention. Before long, the other students were laughing and applauding, even dancing with me.

The nuns didn't know what to do; after all, I was following my punishment to the letter. I had merely turned adversity into opportunity, making my humiliation a celebration. They were appalled, but they should have seen it coming. Earlier in the year, I had been assigned to play the role of a tree in the school play. The director told me to stand still in the back corner of the stage, but that didn't make any sense to me. First of all, how boring! Second of all, a tree needs room for her branches to grow. *If I'm going to be a tree,* I thought, *I'm going to be the biggest tree there is!* So, when the play began, I took my place in the corner, but bit by bit, I danced toward center stage, extending and waving my branches until the scene ended, and I bowed to raucous applause.

After the wastebasket episode, I think the nuns gave up fighting me and decided I was simply incorrigible. They'd just wait me out until I graduated to high school. Looking back, I now understand what I was doing: refusing to stay in the box they put me in. I was challenging that structured world where every moment of my life was scheduled and enforced, with no deviation, no freedom. Now that I've spent my entire career in the close company of some of the world's greatest entrepreneurs, I realize that my childhood behaviors were not much different from many of theirs. Like them, I have always approached the world differently—and I have always felt right in doing so.

QUEEN OF THE CITY

For my high school education, my mother had a different plan. My sisters and I would continue to attend school far from the plantation, but this time, instead of having us board at the school, my mother would buy a home nearby so we could live together—and, no doubt, so she could keep an eye on us. Or, more specifically, on me.

But my most vivid memory of my high school years did not happen in school; it came from a lesson my father taught me in the most unexpected way.

In the town nearest our farm, every year there was a big festival, including a parade honoring that year's Queen of the City. Well, given my love of the spotlight, it's probably no surprise that I wanted that crown—to ride the big parade float and wave to the cheering crowd. True to his character, my father supported me in my dream.

That year, there were three candidates, including me. We spent the day of the festival posing in our makeup and ball gowns, shaking hands, smiling, working hard to charm the crowd. The event was a fundraiser for charity, so throughout the day, people voted for their favorite candidate by making a donation into a collection box with the candidate's name on it. Whoever raised the most money would win the crown. It all came to a climax at a dinner dance where the queen would be announced and the coronation would take place.

One of the other candidates came from an extremely wealthy family, and her father made it clear he was prepared to do whatever it took to make her queen. Throughout the evening, time and again, he would ostentatiously approach her collection box and make a big show of stuffing more money in, taunting the other two fathers.

Meanwhile, to my growing dismay, my father, always so competitive, never even neared my collection box. Instead, he spent the evening socializing with other guests, drinking, telling stories—doing everything, it seemed, but supporting me. Watching him, I grew more disappointed by the moment, resigning myself to being merely a princess. Then, just before the voting closed, someone walked up and dropped a big envelope full of money into my box. The donations were counted, and the winner was announced: I was the Queen of the City.

How did it happen? When I asked my father about it afterward, he explained that, ahead of the dance, he had arranged for someone to keep watch over the donations, tallying the numbers. At the last minute, his proxy was instructed to fill an envelope with enough money to win the crown, then drop it in my box while my father stood casually talking, and apparently unaware, on the other side of the room.

My father did not just win my coronation that night, he showed me what his domino strategies looked like in the real world: don't let your opponent see your plan until you're ready to execute. That's what he had done: he'd lulled his competitor into complacency, then he'd made his move.

Lesson: Don't let your competition in on your plan.

I don't really remember much about my "reign" as Queen of the City, but I've never forgotten that lesson.

SKYWARD

After high school, as was the custom of the time, my younger brothers were expected to go to college, preferably an agricultural institute, to earn degrees in farm management or agronomics and join the family business. We daughters were expected to attend finishing school in Europe, then make a good marriage and settle into family life, raising children and managing a household like the one we grew up in. However, the finishing-school plan derailed soon after my oldest sister, Antonia, arrived at her school in Spain. She got into so much mischief that my father ordered her to come home.

So, with finishing school off the table, I took a few art classes after high school, but as usual, I was restless. Besides, I had no intention of marrying some rich boy and embarking on a lifetime of idle wealth. I wanted to *do* something. But how many career options did women like me have in the Philippines (or, frankly, anywhere) in 1959? One.

Back then, being a "stewardess" was considered a glamorous profession. When you saw a stewardess walking with purpose through the airport, in her crisp uniform and neat cap, you knew she was among the elite, a person in control of her life, out to see the world. No wonder those job openings attracted hundreds of applicants.

Thankfully, the profession was acceptable to my parents, largely because the two-month training was a lot like finishing school. As for me, it appealed to my enduring desire to be in the spotlight, but most of all, it involved my great love: flying. Luckily, I wouldn't be the first in my family to step on this track. My second-oldest sister, Marilen, already had earned a spot with Philippine Airlines. She was great at her job, and she would coach me through the process.

Ironically, not long after I finished my training, my sister left the profession. She had fallen in love and decided to get married, which meant compulsory retirement—only unmarried women could be stewardesses. My sister was ready to settle down and start a family, but I had no such plans. Once I began to work flights, I couldn't imagine any other life. I was just eighteen years old, but already I had found my passion. I loved the fast pace, the responsibility, the excitement of meeting new people and seeing new places. I loved flying to Honolulu, to Hong Kong, to Copenhagen, and exploring those cities during my brief layovers.

I could write an entire book about the experiences I had in the air, but a few stand out among them.

One of my first flights, on a DC-3, was to the Zamboanga Peninsula on the Philippine island of Mindanao. The peninsula features a large city of the same name, but the region was mostly jungle inhabited by native tribal groups.

Veteran flight attendants were accustomed to having some unusual passengers from Zamboanga, but for this newbie, it came as quite a surprise when I looked up to see two tribal warriors, in full regalia, striding down the aisle toward me. Not only that, but each was boldly carrying—despite a sign on the bulkhead near the entry door that read "Please deposit all deadly weapons"—their traditional kris, a double-edged wavy sword. Deadly weapons for sure.

Rules were rules, so I politely asked these passengers if I could take their swords and stow them away. They sternly refused, and no amount of coaxing on my part would change their minds. Finally, not knowing what to do next, I went to the pilot and explained the situation. He seemed unsurprised, and a little amused by my concern. Apparently, among the Zamboanga tribes, a sword is a sign of authority, so, of course, they wouldn't hand theirs over. Obviously, the pilot had seen this kind of thing before, and he gave the okay for the warriors to keep their swords, as long as I kept watch over them. I moved the pair to the last row, next to the galley, and I had my eyes glued on them the entire flight.

Just before landing, as part of our service, we would walk down the aisle handing out candies on a tray. When I reached the warriors, they took the entire tray, along with all of the candies. They looked at me with big, gold-toothed smiles. I believe they thought I was giving them a gift.

As much as I loved it, in-flight service wasn't easy work, and it came with some costs, not least being away from my family. There was also the ever-present risk of air travel. It never entirely left my mind that the most dangerous times were during takeoff and landing, and I wouldn't fully relax until we had touched down and parked at the gate.

One day, I met a stewardess friend at the airport for lunch before we headed out on separate flights to Manila. We had such fun talking that we agreed to meet again later that day after our flights returned. Hers was going to take off just ahead of mine, so we said our goodbyes and she rushed off.

An hour later, I was in my plane, preparing the cabin, when the captain called me up to the cockpit. He told me there had been an emergency—a plane had crashed just beyond the end of the runway. When we were finally cleared for takeoff, we flew over the crash site. The wreckage was still burning below us, and I saw it was my friend's plane. She, and everyone else, had died in the crash. I remember looking out the window in horror and thinking, *Oh my God, this is real. It really can happen. At any time.* I was heartsick, but I stayed on.

On another occasion, while we were in the air, I got a call from the cockpit. The pilot informed me that there was a fire in the belly of the plane. Immediately, I broke out the emergency "bible" and reviewed the instructions for securing the cabin. Then the phone buzzed again: this time, the pilot said he would be attempting a foam landing.

So, there I was, just nineteen years old, marching up and down the aisle, wearing a mask of confidence, ordering passengers to brace for impact—all of those frightened faces looking at me, trusting my abilities. Meanwhile, as I strapped myself into the jump seat, all I could think about was my father, who would be waiting at the airport to pick me up. Whatever happened to that plane—and to me—he would be watching.

In the end, the pilots executed a perfect foam landing. We popped open the doors, and the passengers safely exited on the emergency chutes. No one was hurt.

When I found my father in the airport, he grabbed me as if he were pulling me from the flames and hugged me tightly. "You are not getting back on a plane," he said. "You are resigning right now."

I released myself from his grip, looked him in the eye, and said, "No, I can't." Knowing me the way he did, I don't imagine he was surprised when I turned around, walked straight to the airline office, and told the scheduler, "Put me on the next flight out." If I didn't get on another plane immediately, I knew I would never fly again. That said, the experience did leave a permanent mark on me: even today when I fly, I go through the emergency checklist in my head as the plane makes its final approach.

Other memories from that time are more bittersweet. On one of my last flights, I tended to an older man who boarded in Hawaii, beaming with joy. After many years, he was finally flying home to the Philippines to see his family, and his excitement was infectious. He delighted in telling me his stories, and I delighted in hearing them. Knowing what it meant to miss family, I was thrilled for him.

Then, about an hour after takeoff, he suddenly passed away. I could not believe it—one minute he was there, so fully alive, and then he was gone. The shock of it overwhelmed me. I could hardly function. For the next eight hours, I kept glancing at that sweet man, still in the seat, wrapped in a blanket. My heart ached for his dream, for his family.

That flight taught me two things. At twenty years old, I learned, irrevocably, that life is so fleeting, you must make the most out of every minute. But just as important, I absorbed a truth that has colored the rest of my professional career: service is everything.

That old man was so happy during those last few minutes of his life, not just because his dream was coming true but because he felt welcome and comfortable during the brief time he was in my care.

Lesson: Make your client's satisfaction your greatest joy.

MANAGEMENT

Despite my love of flying, in the end, I only spent two years as a flight attendant. After that, I was promoted to management, to a position called check flight attendant—a job that combined office work with occasional flights during which I assessed new trainees' skills and determined if they met Philippine Airlines' impeccable standards. On every flight I boarded, the crew's response to my presence reminded me of the seriousness of my position—not only was I responsible for maintaining the airline's reputation, I held the trainees' fate in my hands.

This led to some awkward moments, especially when I had to grade my own cousin, who had just finished his steward's training. Unfortunately, he was terrible—so terrible I could not understand how he had gotten that far. It was obvious that he didn't like the passengers, so, of course, his customer service was awful. Family or not, I did what I had to do: I flunked him. He was so angry that he would not speak to me for years, but I knew I had made the right choice for the company. It ended up being the right choice for my cousin, too. After he left the airline, he went into government, eventually becoming a congressman representing his province. Of course, our friendship outlasted that incident. Today, my cousin chuckles, remembering, "I was so angry with you. But you were right." I say, "You're darn right I was right. You shouldn't have been on the flight," and we have a good laugh.

I spent several years as a check flight attendant, learning some crucial skills in leadership and responsibility, including how to find the courage to look beyond sentiment and make tough decisions. Perhaps the toughest decision had to do with one of my best friends, a fellow flight attendant. She had become romantically involved with a married pilot, which was just about the ultimate no-no in our business. According to airline policy of the time, she had to be terminated, and it fell to me to do the terminating. The thought of firing my own friend just killed me. I even wrote to my dad, explaining how torn I was. But, in the end, I did it.

Ultimately, working at the airline was not just my finishing school but the university where I studied humanity. Sometimes, I would arrive at the airport hours before my flight, just to watch people walking by or waiting at their gates. There I began earning my PhD in *people*, with a specialization in understanding each individual's unique needs so I could provide the best possible service to anyone. More than any academic credentials could have, my people studies prepared me for a career I did not yet know I would begin, in a country I never dreamed I would call home.

AN AMERICAN BOY

My romantic life hardly matched the myth associated with stewardesses in those days. Frankly, my flights were so long and the stopovers so brief that I barely had time to get to a hotel, recover from my shift, grab a meal in whatever town I was in, and then rush back to the airport for a flight home. Even Honolulu wasn't that exciting in those days. I remember landing, seeing a couple palm trees, and thinking, *This is it?* Frankly, most of my social life took place in the air, among my coworkers.

By the time I was twenty-four years old, I had dated enough to meet a boy I liked, and we had even become engaged, but it wasn't destined to last. So, my girlfriend—one of the top models in the Philippines, who had a very active social life—took me on as her project, insisting she set me up on a blind date, with an American.

I had never dated an American, and I wasn't really sure I wanted to until she showed me this young man's photo: wearing only bathing trunks and a grin, he was holding a shark he had just caught. Wow. Still, I demurred. "Then come to a party," my friend said. "You can meet him in person and see what you think." I agreed.

When I finally met MarDell in person, I was underwhelmed. Sure, he was tall and in good shape, but he was also fully dressed in rather boring clothes and wearing glasses—hardly the Adonis of the photograph. I made plans for an early exit.

But then something happened. MarDell and I talked. We *really* talked. He was the first man—other than my father—with whom I'd ever had more than a superficial conversation. We spoke about big ideas—our travels, our dreams, our passions. I had been taught that men didn't want to know how smart you were, but MarDell was honestly interested in what I had to say. He took my ideas seriously. Never in my life had I had a conversation like this—substantive and intelligent—with anyone outside my family. I was blown away.

By the end of the party, I knew he was the one.

In my experience, women know who they are going to marry long before the men they are pursuing have a clue. Boy, did I pursue MarDell. I quickly learned that my intended had an adventurous spirit. He explored the Philippines in ways I never would have imagined doing: He trekked through the mountains. He rowed his *bangka*—a small, double-sided outrigger canoe—around the Hundred Islands National Park. He took buses to remote areas where he was likely the first American the residents had ever seen. This tall Caucasian man with the outgoing personality and foreign features—he must have been such a curiosity to them. Anyway, if I wanted to maintain MarDell's interest, I was going to need to keep up with him. I may have questioned his sanity while hiking steep trails in sweltering heat, thinking, *Who the heck goes hiking in the Philippines?* I may have come home from our dates aching and exhausted, but spending time with MarDell was always exhilarating, and by seeing the land through his eyes, I opened up my world.

Along the way, we talked about poetry, philosophy, jazz, and world affairs. But MarDell never said much about his work. I knew he was an army officer stationed at Clark Air Base in Manila. Beyond that, I knew nothing—and probably for good reason. Years later, I would find out MarDell worked in intelligence, monitoring and decoding the radio signals emanating from the other side in the war in Vietnam.

There were definitely some clues that my boyfriend was a spy. For instance, whenever I tried to call him at the base, I was told that he was in a briefing. Eventually, MarDell told me those phone calls of mine nearly got him in big trouble—his work was so sensitive that he was not allowed to date a Philippine national.

Eight months into our courtship, I discovered just how secret his work was when I finally arranged for MarDell to join me at my family home to meet my parents. A day after he arrived from Manila, he came down with acute appendicitis and had to be rushed to the hospital for

emergency surgery—they needed to operate before his appendix rup-
tured. Despite the urgency, the hospital could not administer anes-
thesia until an official from the US consulate arrived to monitor the
procedure, to keep MarDell from talking while sedated. I remember
thinking, *Hmm, that's strange,* but I honestly didn't give it much more
thought.

I had other concerns to deal with. Thanks to my mother, I was
raised a strict Roman Catholic. MarDell was a lapsed Mormon. To
marry outside my faith was potentially a bigger scandal to my family
than my marrying an American spy. Worse, marrying a non-Catholic
would disqualify me from having my wedding in a Catholic church—a
heartbreak for my mother and for me. I didn't know what to do.

As it happened, on one of the last flights I worked before retiring,
we had a most unusual passenger on board: Bishop Fulton J. Sheen, a
Catholic leader known worldwide for his radio show, *The Catholic Hour,*
and his television program, *Life Is Worth Living.* Well, being me, at my
first opportunity, I struck up a conversation with this great man, who
was headed to the Philippines to celebrate the Bicentennial Jubilee, a
special year focused on the remission of sins and universal pardon.

The bishop was exactly as you would imagine—calm, thought-
ful, and wise. Amused by my presumption, he asked me about myself,
and I immediately blurted out what was so deeply troubling me: that
my mother, who was a woman of deep Catholic faith and charity, had
always dreamed that I would be married in the local church that she
had been so instrumental in building. But that was not possible unless
I could get a special dispensation from the church.

His Excellency listened intently. He asked for my name, which
his assistant wrote down. Then, right there in the aisle of the plane, I
knelt, and Bishop Fulton J. Sheen gave me his blessing. It was a surreal
moment but also deeply comforting: my dilemma wasn't resolved, but
I knew a revered leader of my church had listened to my concerns and
blessed me.

A few weeks later, my mother received the most wonderful surprise: a notice from the Archdiocese of Manila. A dispensation had
been granted, and I was free to marry in our church. The bishop had
given me my miracle.

I still had one more obstacle to overcome: my father. He had known almost from the start that I was romantically involved with a US Army officer, but he didn't think it was serious. Even when MarDell's and my devotion to one another became obvious, my father seemed in denial. He never discussed it with others; he never talked about it with me. I suspect he was hoping this binational romance would fade away, as had my other boyfriends over the years.

Ironically, my father did to himself exactly what he had done to competitors over the years—he kept himself deluded until it was too late to react. By the time his delusion broke, I had obtained the dispensation from the church, my mother had begun making arrangements, and MarDell had returned from Manila to ask my father's blessing.

"It will never work," he told MarDell. "You two are from completely different cultures," he said, somehow ignoring the counterarguments of those two ancestral portraits hanging in the hallway, of his own Spanish heritage and my mother's Filipino Swiss lineage.

When this approach didn't work on MarDell, my father played his trump card: "My daughter," he told my fiancé, "was raised in luxury. It is the only world she knows. What are you taking her to, in that alien place across the ocean? The impoverished, gypsy life of a low-ranking military officer? Do you think she'll ever be happy with that? Do you think you'll ever be able to give her the life she was bred for?"

To MarDell's eternal credit, he was neither intimidated nor persuaded. "We love each other," he told my father, "and I will take care of her."

My father may have been a very competitive man, but he also knew when he had lost—and how to be a gracious loser. He surrendered and gave us his blessing.

Only one concern remained. MarDell's army tour ended before we planned to be married, which meant he had to return to the United States. Though I never so much as whispered a word of worry to my family, I had heard too many stories of GIs promising to marry local girls, then leaving for America, never to return. *What if?* I could barely allow myself to think about it, though the question fluttered at my heart like a moth at a light bulb.

MarDell, of course, was good to his word. He returned to the Philippines and we had a lovely wedding, with my brothers and sisters in attendance, my mother weeping tears of joy, and my father, whatever his inner thoughts, looking on with pride.

Then it was time to go. Beyond the hole in the clouds, America beckoned.

CHAPTER 2

NEWCOMER

Our honeymoon took us directly from the Philippines to Copenhagen and Rome. Having traveled to Europe many times before, I had expected to enjoy the creature comforts of the hotels I had stayed in as a flight attendant. Our honeymoon proved a rude awakening—and a glimpse of my life to come. It wasn't MarDell's fault. He wanted to give me the European vacation of my dreams, but our timing was off—recently discharged from the army, he hadn't yet landed a job back home. We simply couldn't afford that trip. His solution: the then-popular bestseller *Europe on Five Dollars a Day.*

Needless to say, Europe was a lot cheaper in 1963, but not *that* cheap. Because of MarDell's intelligence background, we had to avoid certain countries during our travels, so we had already used a big chunk of our savings on a complicated multi-stop flight itinerary. As a result, when we finally arrived, and for the weeks that followed, that little paperback became MarDell's bible, determining exactly where we were going to stay, where we were going to eat, and how much we were going to spend.

It's a good thing we were in love because our honeymoon budget alone was an endurance test. We would walk miles, past wonderful restaurants, to get to that one cheap café listed in the book. We lugged our own suitcases up narrow hotel staircases and slept in cramped

rooms, on lumpy beds, with shared toilets down the hall. I was con-
tinuously tired, starving, and—because I was so used to getting my
way—complaining. I must have been a real challenge for MarDell, but
remarkably, he remained unflappable and single-mindedly focused on
meeting the five-dollar-a-day challenge while exploring the treasures
those beautiful cities had to offer us for free—the art, the history, the
music, the architecture.

So, there we were, wandering through Rome—the Colosseum,
Vatican City, Trevi Fountain, the Pantheon—and all I could think
was, *I'm hungry. I'm hungry. I'm hungry.* If I told MarDell, he'd say,
"Okay, well, let me look at the book." Inevitably, he'd find some cheap
restaurant forty minutes away by foot—of course, taxis were out of the
question. I'd whine, point to the restaurant right across the street, deli-
cious aromas pouring out its front door, and say, "Well, why don't we
just go to this restaurant right here?" He'd reply, "It's not in the book.
It's going to cost too much." So, I trudged along, loving my brilliant,
adventurous, determined, endlessly patient husband but hating that
stupid book. That's when it dawned on me: *Oh my God, this is just what
my dad warned me about. Being on a budget. Being poor. Now I know
what he meant.*

NEWLYWEDS

MarDell and I began our married life in Upland, California, a small
town on the freeway between Los Angeles and San Bernardino. Once
famous for its endless orange groves and fruit orchards, Upland was a
nice middle-class town, which MarDell chose because he had worked
in a factory there one summer, and he felt the job prospects would be
good.

Here the reality of my married life truly set in. I was a new bride in
a new country, surrounded by new sights, sounds, smells, and flavors.
I had to familiarize myself with a new dialect of English. I had to learn
the customs of suburban life while figuring out how to be the wife
of a working man who himself was struggling to develop his career.
Nothing in my upbringing had prepared me for this. I had never set
foot in the kitchen of my childhood home, much less learned to cook.

My laundry had always been washed, ironed, and put away for me. Running a household, on a budget, was nowhere on my list of skills. A clear sign that I had not understood what I was getting myself into when I prepared for this move: among the belongings I had shipped to the United States from the Philippines were several trunks filled with evening gowns.

Nevertheless, here we were. MarDell quickly found a job at an assembly plant, and we rented a one-bedroom apartment on the second floor of a small building, which we furnished with a big yellow couch and two chairs. The kitchen was tiny, but it had great windows through which I watched MarDell leave for work in the morning and come back home at night. For the first few weeks, that is what I did: stayed in the apartment, alone, looking out the window, fearful of going out in a strange land, and counting the hours until MarDell returned.

Looking back, those were the loneliest days of my life—no family, no friends, no exciting career, just this foreign land and not the vaguest sense of how I fit into it.

But I've never been a person to hide from the world for long. Soon enough, I made my first friend in America. She was an unlikely choice—or more accurately, I was an unlikely choice for her—but she introduced herself while I was walking up the staircase from the parking lot to our apartment, and I jumped on the opportunity to make a friend.

She was, in fact, the owner of our building, and she lived in an apartment below us. As near as I could tell, she spent most of the day drinking beer, smoking cigarettes, and watching Roller Derby. We couldn't have been more different. I had come from half a world away, and she, by comparison, was as American as could be. She was much older than me—probably in her seventies—and looked as though her hardscrabble life was the only one she had ever known. Underneath her rough exterior, she was a wonderfully kind person, and that native kindness led her to bring me under her wing.

Each day, she would climb the stairs, wearing a housecoat, with a cigarette dangling from her lips, knock on my door, and say, "Honey, it's time." I would follow her down to her apartment, and we'd sit there watching Roller Derby while she drank her beer and chain-smoked. We'd talk about the bout on TV, about the news, about local gossip, and anything else she thought interesting. She would give me advice: where to buy groceries, how to take the bus, how to use American slang (I learned all the profanities listening to her yell at the TV). She knew she was my only friend, and she made it her mission to help me acclimate to life in the States.

When I wasn't in my friend's apartment, I was in my own, trying to play the role of a good wife. I was particularly obsessed with ironing. Before I came to America, I had never touched an iron. Now, alone for the day in Upland, I got so excited about doing something domestic that I spent a whole afternoon perfecting the art of putting a crease in MarDell's trousers. When he came home that night, I was so excited to show him. He stifled his amusement, but his reaction made it clear: I'd done it wrong. Ever gentle with his fish-out-of-water wife, he said to me, "This is *excellent*. But you put in so much work on this. I don't want you to work so hard. Next time, you don't have to do the crease."

Wasn't that nicely done? He could have just said, "Good Lord, don't ever do that again," but that wasn't MarDell's way.

MarDell taught me many things—including how to iron properly and how to cook—but the most important thing he taught me was how to stay calm. He was almost superhuman in his patience toward me, and I could be very trying. He did, however, draw the line when this young woman who grew up in a world of "yes" needed to learn the meaning of "no." Once we went to a restaurant, and I didn't like the food I'd ordered. I told MarDell I wanted to order something else. He asked, "Is there something wrong with it?"

"No," I replied, "I just want something different."

Without a hint of frustration, he informed me, "No, you just ordered this. You must have thought about it. You decided that was what you wanted. So, now you need to eat it."

I thought, *What?* In my parents' house, I would have politely asked for a different dish, and moments later, it would appear. Not anymore. I was beginning to realize how I had lived in a bubble my whole life and how it was time to learn to live like everyone else.

In contrast to MarDell's indefatigable patience, I had always had a temper. In this strange new place, with all its frustrations and sacrifices, that temper regularly surfaced. One evening, while we were eating dinner at home, I got into a tiff with MarDell, and in a fit of pique, I picked up my bowl of spaghetti and threw it against the wall. MarDell didn't say anything. He just looked at me with an expression that said, "What do you do with a spoiled child?" Then he picked up *his* bowl and flung it against the same wall. The two of us stood there in disbelief, watching spaghetti sauce drip down the wall—and we burst out laughing. We cleaned up the mess together, having forgotten what had triggered my explosion in the first place. I can't say that was my temper's final appearance, but over time, MarDell's composure rubbed off on me.

Eventually, my husband's Mensa-level language skills would help me, too. As any non-native English speaker will tell you, developing fluency in English is no easy task. In the Philippines, I had learned English in school, and I had spoken it with passengers when I was an airline attendant, but that was formal English, not everyday American speech. Remember, on my father's orders, my family spoke Spanish at the dinner table, and in my interactions with our household staff, neighbors, and people in town, I spoke local dialects, of which there are well over a hundred in the Philippines. I was fluent in three of them. So, until I met MarDell, English was a small fraction of my daily language.

Now, for weeks on end, it was the only language I would hear or speak. Practicing with my neighbor friend helped me smooth out my stilted sentences, but a lot of the words she taught me weren't for polite conversation. It was MarDell who accelerated my full entry into American life by helping me develop my conversational skills and answering my seemingly endless questions about American idioms that boggled my mind. Eventually I became as fast-talking as any American, though I never did let go of my accent.

Even with all this learning going on, after those first lonely weeks in Upland, I grew bored of my routine: watching Roller Derby, attempting house chores, and waiting at the window for MarDell to come home. So, I resolved to expand my horizons. MarDell walked me through using the bus system, and though I was nervous at first, freedom beckoned. I came to love traveling about, seeing how my new neighbors lived.

Once I was comfortable going out, MarDell made it his project to teach me how to operate in the big world. Our budget was not as tight as on our honeymoon, but MarDell's factory job didn't leave us with much extra; plus, he was paying tuition for night classes to advance in his career. To lighten his load, I needed to take on more responsibilities. So, on weekends, MarDell and I would go to the supermarket together, and he would give me lessons in bargain shopping. I remember standing in front of an entire display case filled with different brands of mayonnaise. His plan was to get me to the point where I could do all of our shopping—and that meant I had to adhere to our budget, which, in turn, meant I had to learn comparison shopping. Our lesson began with mayonnaise.

"Okay," he said, "what's the best buy here?"

I picked the one in front of me and held it up for his approval.

"No, you have to figure out the ounces," he said, taking it from my hand and returning it to the shelf.

The ounces? I wondered. *What is that?* Of course, I was capable of learning anything I wanted to learn, but did I really care to learn *this*? I felt like I was back in boarding school, being forced to complete all the steps when really I just wanted to jump to step ten. Ultimately, I did learn to factor price per ounce, because I had to, but to this day, I still can't stand to comparison shop.

Just as MarDell and I were settling into our new routines, my mother and father announced that they were coming for a visit. Both, I suspect, but especially my father, had real doubts about my ability to pull off this new life, and true to form, they wanted to check up on me. Of course, they also wanted to help in any way they could, which started with renting an apartment next to us for a couple months. I was so grateful for their company, and so ready to show them the ways I had adapted so far—little did I know, they would take it upon themselves to adapt, too.

My mother did everything she could to extend her warmth and kindness to MarDell. I would overhear her trying to communicate with him in English, then she'd pull me aside and say, "Okay, talk to your husband, because I am running out of English words." Always, my mother had delighted in the world—amazed by every new wonder, and my new environment offered her plenty of those. Watching her take it all in—she was adorable, her enthusiasm infectious.

For his part, my father seemed to take great joy in carrying out the most mundane tasks. His assignment was to take out the garbage—a chore he would never do at home. Sometimes he would get so excited about his daily task that he'd show up early in the morning to announce, "Okay, I'm ready for the garbage!" Then he'd make a big show of preparing the bag and hauling it to the dumpster.

The most gratifying part of my parents' visit, though, was watching my father and MarDell plant the seeds of a lifelong friendship. Over a game of dominoes or chess, those two would talk for hours. Listening to their two brilliant minds moving from one topic to the next, punctuated by fits of laughter, it was like hearing two instruments play a whole symphony. Apparently, my father had left his strict demeanor in the Philippines. Here in the United States, he became the father I'd met during those flights above our province, the one who showed up carefree and dancing in Spain. Watching the two most important men in my life bond like this—it felt like all was right in my world. For the moment.

Six months after my parents returned to the Philippines, my mother died of cancer. Her absence sent a painful shock through our family, the plantation, and my heart. Though my father and I had always shared a special bond, my mother's influence on me ran deep. By example, she taught me to listen attentively, to really try to understand people, to treat everyone with kindness, and to appreciate the wonders of this world, big and small. In the Philippines, there was a great disparity between the privileged class and the people who worked on the farms and in the households. Unlike many people in her position, my mother carried her good fortune as a mandate to help others who were less well-off. She is the one who turned our household into a village, caring for the well-being of everyone who lived and worked there. To this day, there is no one who speaks of my mother without a smile. Hers is a legacy I am proud to carry on.

SILICON VALLEY

MarDell discovered a new career path in Upland, and we followed it up north, to San José State University, where he had been accepted into the mechanical engineering program. There we landed in a tiny studio apartment, in the fast-growing city of San Jose. Now that MarDell was attending school full-time, I needed to bring some money into our household. But how?

This wasn't a new question. On my father's first visit to Upland, though my parents certainly saw how I'd grown since I had left home, my father, ever the dominoes player, ever looking five moves ahead before taking his next step, wanted me to do more. One morning, he had pulled me aside and said, "You need to be independent. You *must* be independent. If something happens to me, or to MarDell, you need to be able to earn a living."

The urgency in his voice—it got my attention, though I couldn't have imagined making any more changes to my life right then. Everything was already so new. Apparently, my father also had shared his concern with MarDell, who wholeheartedly agreed—I needed to be secure, with or without him. I think both men understood something else about me, too: once the novelty and challenge of acclimation subsided, I was going to get bored. I was, by nature, someone who needed action, stimulation, change. Of course, I would have been perfectly happy to delay employment until that boredom kicked in, but now our student budget was forcing the issue, and the question came back around: What could I do to make money?

As I saw it, I had no skills. I was raised to be a socialite, a wealthy man's wife, to live a life of leisure accented by charity work. MarDell recognized something different in me. While we were dating, he had observed me at work—he saw how I managed people, how devoted I was to service, how adept I was at understanding people's wants and needs. So, MarDell suggested door-to-door sales—after all, there were no barriers to entry, and weren't sales a lot like customer service? So, I signed up with Avon, a cosmetics company, as I knew something about perfume.

Now remember, at Philippine Airlines, I had received such rigorous training that when I finally donned my uniform, I felt confident working as part of a crew, in a role I absolutely loved. But selling cosmetics, by myself, to strangers, in their homes? I had neither confidence nor love for this profession.

Nonetheless, MarDell appointed himself my sales coach, role-playing sales calls to show me how it was done. I would step outside the apartment and ring the doorbell, and he would open the door as a different person each time. He would be friendly—*too* friendly—or angry or rude or distracted. Sometimes he would shout and terrify me. I never knew what to expect. Other times, I would just start crying, aggravated that I had to do this at all. But MarDell would say, "This is exactly what you can expect." He was right. It was good training because I never knew what was going to happen when the door opened.

I never really had to hit the streets on my own like a proper Avon Lady, though. Typically, MarDell would drive me around a neighborhood. He'd stop and say, "This looks like a good house." I wouldn't want to get out of the car. MarDell would announce firmly, "You can do this. You gotta go. Go now." Clearly, he believed in me more than I did. That was the thing about MarDell—he dispatched challenges and encouragement in equal measure. Reluctantly, I would leave the car, trembling as I knocked on the door.

I'd like to say that I proved to be a natural saleswoman, but in fact, I was terrible. I may have been the worst Avon Lady in history. I never sold a single item. Because we had to first buy those items to sell, I have the unique distinction of *losing* money as a door-to-door salesperson. My bottom line as an Avon salesperson was red.

Scratch those career plans.

But I was still intent on finding a job. Next, I took advantage of the Christmas season and got a job gift wrapping at the Macy's in San Jose's Westfield Valley Fair mall. It didn't take long for me to realize that I not only hated gift wrapping but I was also really bad at it. I still pity those shoppers who had to look at my handiwork under their Christmas trees.

Through it all, I dreamed of getting back to the career I loved: flying. However, as a married woman, that door was closed to me. But I had stayed in touch with my old girlfriends, many of whom still worked for the airlines. One day, I met a friend who was on a layover for lunch, and I shared my situation. She suggested, "Why don't you become a travel agent?"

It was an epiphany. *Why not?*

My dad was visiting at the time, so I showed him a want ad from a travel agency in the local newspaper, and I asked him to drive me to their office, a few miles away, in Sunnyvale. There I encountered the most unlikely coincidence. The owner of the travel agency proved to be a rather unpleasant guy—but, though he was American, he had once been the manager of a Dole pineapple farm in the Philippines. When he learned my family history, he offered me a job. It was kismet. Better yet, because I reminded him of his old life, I became his protégé.

I was on my way.

It was a strange experience. On the one hand, he taught me a lot about the travel business. But on the other hand, he was a terrible businessman. I don't think he needed the money, so the agency was just a kind of hobby to him. His indifference to its success translated into indifference toward his customers. He would *yell* at them. I couldn't believe it. In the airline industry, this would be a firing offense.

That's when I started a mental list: all the things I would do differently if I ever had my own agency. I resolved to always be attentive to my customers. I resolved to create an environment where people would feel happy to be at work, not horrified by their boss's behavior. I also began looking around for a new job.

In a way, you could say my first boss taught me an important lesson—if only to do just the opposite of him.

TAKING CONTROL

I lasted a year at that travel agency until I couldn't take it anymore. It was now the mid-sixties, and much had changed in my life. I had grown accustomed to America, even the fast-moving, high-rolling world of what would soon be called Silicon Valley. Not that I knew much about the technology companies popping up around me—I was focused on selling airline tickets to individual clients. Nevertheless, I now moved independently through my day: walking from our apartment to the train station in Downtown San Jose, riding for four miles, getting off at the Sunnyvale station, then walking a mile to the travel office—and reversing the process at the end of the workday. I was also growing more ambitious. One day at lunch, I visited an art gallery and fell in love with a painting. It was bold. It showed a wooded area, with a dirt path leading off into the distance. I had to have it. But it cost $40—the equivalent of $325 today—which I didn't have. So, I spoke to the owner and reached an agreement that I would pay monthly installments of five dollars. It took eight months, but I finally paid it off. It was a pretty big painting, and I remember tucking it under my arm and lugging it a mile through downtown Sunnyvale and onto the train. I must have made a pretty amusing sight. But I didn't care; I had my painting. That painting hangs in my bedroom today, more than half a century later. I look at its path into the unknown whenever I have to make a big decision. It reminds me of a belief that has guided me for ages.

Lesson: Once you make a decision, assume you chose the right path. Second-guessing only gets in your way.

MarDell by now had graduated from San José State and found work at Lockheed Missiles and Space, which was also in Sunnyvale, close enough for him to take me to lunch sometimes. Those were lovely lunches, but the rest of the time, I was stuck in that two-person travel agency, in the middle of endless shouting matches between unhappy customers and a grouchy owner.

On the weekends, MarDell and I would grab a couple sleeping bags, fill a duffel bag with the bare essentials, throw them in the back of our car—a Peugeot we named Buena Suerte, or Good Luck—and drive up to the Russian River for a campout. That was it: no tent, no folding chairs, no pillows. Just our two sleeping bags, laid out on the ground, under a canopy of stars. The scenery was beautiful, but I have to admit, after a couple nights sleeping on the rocky ground, I didn't really mind when Monday rolled around.

Despite the miserable job environment, I found I liked the work. Not to mention that the owner, despite his many flaws, did take the time to teach me some important skills, including making travel reservations, airline ticketing, and routing. So, when applying for my next job, I had a diverse portfolio of skills. I got the job, and better yet, it was in San Jose. No more commuting.

Unfortunately, the bread-and-butter business of this agency wasn't airline travel but selling bus tickets to Las Vegas for gamblers and tourists. It was steady work, but it wasn't for me. Almost from my first day on the job, I started looking for a new employer. Somehow, unconsciously, I already had absorbed the Silicon Valley career trajectory: keep moving, always in search of the next opportunity.

I soon found another agency in San Jose, this one largely handling corporate accounts. It seemed ideal, so I applied—and now, thanks to my growing résumé, I got the job.

Why, after these first two unrewarding jobs, didn't I just give up on travel and try a different profession? I think it was a combination of my love for flying and my natural unwillingness to accept failure. I just kept telling myself, *Maybe this new job will be the one.* That *this time it will work.* Though I had not yet found the ideal workplace, I sensed that, at its best, this profession could combine all the things I had loved most about being a flight attendant—connecting with people, understanding their wants and needs, and creating wonderful experiences for them. Besides, after my adventures with door-to-door selling and gift wrapping, I wasn't sure I could *do* anything else.

My new employer, Travel Planners, was based just a few blocks from Downtown San Jose, which gave me my first sustained taste of urban life. It was a relatively small agency—though bigger than I was used to—with six employees. It was owned by a husband-and-wife team— he was from England and she from Mexico—but the real boss was the gentleman's sister, and she was fabulous. I learned so much from her in the months that followed. Because of her, our relatively new agency enjoyed a tremendous burst of growth—to thirty employees—during the six years I was there. I would soon learn that this doubling in size every year was a benchmark for success in the emerging digital age.

Travel Planners was, in fact, two travel businesses. Upstairs handled corporate accounts; downstairs took care of vacation planning. I managed a couple vacation accounts, including one for two Italian gentlemen who came in regularly to book big, lavish trips, always paying in cash. I found them to be delightful—articulate, well dressed, polite—but my coworkers seemed scared of them. Later I would find out why: they were members of the Mafia. Aside from those two clients, I was assigned to upstairs, where I arranged corporate travel for fascinating new tech companies with big plans to transform the world—a stroke of luck that changed my life forever.

Among those new companies, one stood out: Intel. At the time, I knew nothing about electronics, much less semiconductors, but I understood this company had a buzz about it. Though they had fewer than one hundred employees, they were growing at a tremendous rate, not to mention that they seemed to be getting an unusual amount of press coverage. Even with my limited view of the tech world, I could tell they were *the* company to watch. Developing this sixth sense—this ability to identify the next hot company—would help me enormously in the coming years.

The single most important piece of knowledge that I had picked up during my apprenticeship with my previous two employers, underscored during my time at Travel Planners, was that with corporate accounts your real client was not the boss taking the trip, but his—and again, they were all men—executive secretary. She—and yes, they were all women—was the key. When you perform well, she looks good, and she will trust you with all future travel reservations for her boss, business and personal.

As it happened, at Intel, my executive client was Andy Grove, who at that point was only a general manager. I sensed that he was going places, as was Intel, but I could never have imagined that Intel would become the most valuable manufacturing company worldwide, and Andy admired as one of the greatest business executives of the twentieth century. At the time, to me, he was just a tough client— one to whom I never spoke directly, and one who, according to Sue McFarland, Andy's executive secretary, was unforgiving of mistakes.

With our common cause of keeping Andy happy, Sue and I became close friends. I worked doubly hard for her, checking and double-checking everything, making myself available at all hours, quickly making last-minute changes, and navigating every logistical or bureaucratic obstacle, all to make sure that Andy Grove enjoyed a smooth, uneventful trip. Sue and I came to trust and depend upon each other. That's one reason we survived for years working for the man who would come to be known as the most intimidating person in Silicon Valley—and he had no shortage of competitors for that title.

A GROWING CONFIDENCE

By now, after eight years of marriage, I was no longer the spoiled young newlywed, fearful of the foreign world outside my window. I had grown confident living in California. MarDell and I were engaged in our careers, and our frugal lifestyle was changing. We dined out and traveled without the shackles of a *Five Dollars a Day* book holding us back. Our adventures expanded beyond weekend road trips spent sleeping on the rocky ground. Instead of challenging me to comparison shop, MarDell was now challenging me to keep up with him on the ski slopes. My God, the first ski lesson he gave me—he had me bundled up in so many layers, I felt like a mummy. "How am I going to learn to ski?" I asked him. "I can't even move!" But MarDell always found a way to make things possible for me. He'd break it down into the littlest steps—let's just see if you can move your arms; let's see if we can get your foot in your boots; let's see if I can adjust the straps to make your boots more comfortable. It must have taken an hour before I managed to click my boot into the binding without falling over. Sure enough, little by little, with unending patience, MarDell coaxed me along, and as usual, I not only figured it out but came to enjoy spending a day on the slopes.

As for work, the Travel Planners job and my new corporate clients confirmed what I had suspected—the qualities that had helped me succeed as a flight attendant were helping me succeed as a travel agent. I was developing a sense of purpose and pride, and my true personality was resurfacing. I even had my own driver's license and car. I couldn't wait to show my father how far I'd come.

On his next visit, I really set out to impress him. He had always been a fan of the Los Angeles Dodgers, listening to their games on the ham radio in the Philippines. So, when he arrived in San Jose, I had a surprise waiting for him: I took him to LA to attend his first major league ball game.

As a measure of my growing independence, MarDell stayed behind while my father and I flew to Southern California on our own. At the airport, I hailed a cab that brought us to Dodgers Stadium. If that wasn't enough to show him how comfortable his daughter had become, I had more in store for him. He didn't know it yet, but I had created not just a trip but an experience for him. He was thrilled just to be at the game, but he became ecstatic when, during the sixth inning, his name came up on the scoreboard, welcoming him to the stadium.

But that wasn't all. I also had talked to Dodgers' management and arranged for my father to meet with two of his favorite players. I knew they were good players, but I didn't realize they were future Hall of Famers. My father certainly knew all about Don Drysdale and Sandy Koufax—a giant man and a small man, both very kind to this fan visiting from far away. He was awestruck. I think he was also relieved: the daughter that had worried him so had not only survived in her new life but was now beginning to thrive.

START-UP

Indeed, MarDell and I had so much to be happy about in those days, except for one thing: my job. I loved the work. I loved my clients and the executive assistants with whom I worked. But—and this seemed endemic to the travel business—Travel Planners, like my two employers before it, just didn't treat its employees well. Again, I found myself taking mental notes of what I *wouldn't* do if I had my own agency someday.

That someday came sooner than I expected. As my frustration grew, I began to discuss the idea of leaving with another agent, Lee Michaels, who worked downstairs in vacation travel. We would eat lunch together, dreaming up the type of enlightened, customer-centric agency we would create one day. Then we'd look at each other and say, "Why don't we just go out on our own?"

At night, I would talk about my frustrations and ideas with MarDell. He not only understood, but he may have been more enthusiastic about my dreams than I was. He knew how good I was at my job—and he also knew how aggravated I had become. "Yeah," he said, "go on your own, you guys. I know you will make it work." He could empathize because he was, I later learned, experiencing his own yearning for career independence.

Ultimately, it was MarDell's enthusiasm and my own growing desperation that propelled me to make my move. That, and one last infuriating event at Travel Planners.

The agency regularly received free airline tickets, which agents could request to use. Well, I wanted to go home to visit my family, so I put in a request for a single ticket, and the owner turned me down with no explanation. That was frustrating enough, but then he turned around and gave all the tickets to his family, leaving none for the employees. That was the last straw. Any hesitation I had to take the entrepreneurial leap disappeared completely. That day, Lee and I quit. Our departure came as a total surprise to the agency—tellingly, they had no idea we were unhappy. We gave no warning, we gave no two weeks' notice, we told no one our plans—we had no intention of sharing our business strategy with a future competitor, nor did we want to upset them by stealing clients. We simply resigned and walked out.

We were free.

CHAPTER 3

ENTREPRENEUR

In 1973, a month after we walked out of Travel Planners, my new business partner and I signed a lease on an office space and started our new company: Travel Experience, a name Lee chose.

As we took stock of our situation, we realized that we had our freedom, yes, but we didn't have much else. Aside from the $1,500 we each contributed for start-up costs, we had no capital. We had no employees. We had no clients. Our sudden departure from Travel Planners had shocked everyone, including the people with whom we had spent years developing positive relationships. We had done almost too good of a job keeping our move quiet. Even if our former clients had wanted to find us, they would not know where to look.

What had seemed like such a noble strategy upon our departure left us thoroughly unprepared to launch Travel Experience. In a single day, we had gone from a client portfolio that included some of the region's most successful companies and individuals to a blank client list. All of our efforts to build our reputations were for naught, because we had made the decision not to poach from our former employer. We weren't just starting from scratch; we were starting from zero.

As you can probably appreciate about me by now, I didn't see our dire situation as a defeat but as a challenge. I may have been the worst

Avon saleswoman of all time, but at least I had experience in door-to-door cold calls. So that's what I did.

I targeted as my territory a new business park in Santa Clara, across the Bayshore Freeway from Intel and surrounding the popular Great America theme park. This property was currently the hottest commercial real estate in Silicon Valley, attracting all of the fast-growing tech start-ups. I knew many would fade away eventually, but some might become the next Hewlett-Packard or Intel. Either way, for now, they would all be buying airline tickets—and they probably hadn't yet found a travel agency.

So, I hit the sidewalks of that business park—or more accurately, because most of the places featured trendy grass berms rather than sidewalks, I walked the streets. Lee and I joked that we must have been Santa Clara's first streetwalkers. Those were long, hot days, traversing the steaming asphalt from building to building, and usually all I accomplished was to leave a newly printed business card with a polite but confused receptionist. I always made a point to dress nicely, including high heels—so by the end of each day, my feet were killing me. But I refused to be defeated.

One miserable day, as I was walking past endless, nearly identical concrete tilt-up office buildings, their signs emblazoned with odd, technical-sounding names, one of my heels suddenly snapped off. Exasperated, I stopped to pull off my shoes and walk barefoot. As I did, I glanced over at the office building beside me. A man sitting in the corner office was looking at me, his expression a mix of amusement and curiosity.

I didn't recognize the man, but I thought, *This is the first actual executive I've encountered in days.* I decided to go in. The name on the sign read "ROLM Corporation." I walked barefoot through the glass doors into the air-conditioned lobby and strode up to the receptionist. "There's a gentleman in the corner office over there," I announced, pointing. "I'd like to speak to him."

You must remember, this was the old Silicon Valley—a much more casual place, where everyone knew each other, and deals were often made with just a handshake. The receptionist was very friendly, but she was obliged to ask, "Do you have an appointment?"

"No," I told her.

"Okay," she replied. "Let me check."

A few minutes later, the man in the window appeared in the lobby, looking for me. It was Ken Oshman, the *O* in ROLM, the name of which would soon be stamped on office phone systems across the globe. Ken was very gracious to me, and he certainly didn't have to be to some brazen woman who had stormed his company's lobby and demanded to meet him. In the end, I didn't get the account—at least not then, but a few years later, ROLM did hire me to manage the travel for one of their corporate retreats. As I became more of a Valley figure, I found myself socializing with Ken and his wife, as well as ROLM's *L*, Walter Loewenstern, and Karen, his wife. But I'm getting ahead of myself.

My limited success with Ken Oshman gave me the courage to go on. Pushing myself to walk through the next door, I would flash back to my Avon experiences and coach myself as MarDell had done: *Okay, you can do this. You've done it before. Just remember: When the door opens, you never know who's going to be there. They could become the biggest client you've ever had.* When that didn't work, I reminded myself that this was now *my* company, I was responsible to my partner for getting corporate accounts, and I couldn't let her down.

Meanwhile, when I wasn't pounding the pavement, Lee and I worked on our office, a two-room suite in Los Altos—an upscale zip code for that tiny space on Distel Drive, overlooking busy El Camino Real, with its fast-food restaurants, bars, and car repair shops. We were so broke that we filled the space with potted ferns to make up for the fact that we had little furniture besides two old Santa Clara University desks bought from Repo Depot for twenty-five dollars each, some worn-out chairs, and a pair of phones that never rang.

What our office did have was an intriguing neighbor, on the tony side of El Camino Real. Her name was Sandra Kurtzig, and she was one of the pioneering woman entrepreneurs in tech. Sandy, who was about my age, had already built a multimillion-dollar software company called ASK Group, Inc. Her company had taken off like a rocket after Hewlett-Packard had chosen ASK's MANMAN computer-aided manufacturing software for its minicomputers.

To finagle a meeting with my neighbor, all I had to do was cross El Camino, from the poverty side to the success side. We met in Sandy's office. I was impressed, not just by how elegant the surroundings were but by Sandy herself. She was tough and smart but also very feminine. She hadn't given an inch to the Valley's male engineering culture. She was as good as any of them, and she knew it. Rather than cater to the young boys' club, she made her own rules and made them respect her. Her bright-red Ferrari Testarossa broadcast her success, and her signature red fingernails punctuated her fierceness.

What nails! I couldn't help staring at them. They were not only fiery red but spectacularly long. When I asked her about pricing strategies and how she got clients to agree to her numbers, she explained by flashing those nails. "If I get the price I want, I smile and touch my hair," she said. "But if they give me a number I don't like, out come *these*," and she rapped those blood-red nails on her desk, a sound equally as intimidating as a man's big fist pounding a table.

I didn't get Sandy Kurtzig's business, either—at least not yet, but I learned something important from her.

Lesson: Be yourself, whoever you are. Make your perceived weakness your strength.

I'd like to say that I ultimately became a huge success at door-to-door selling this time around. Instead, I maintained my record as a cold-calling saleswoman: a perfect zero. I didn't land a single client. I tried to console myself by saying that I had made a lot of contacts, notably among those all-important secretaries and receptionists. Indeed, in the months and years to come, my relationships with those women would pay exponential dividends. But in those early weeks, meeting them did nothing for our bottom line. Lee had struggled, too, but at least she had brought in some individual clients. I had nothing—and she couldn't help me because she knew nothing about the commercial market. It was up to me alone, and I was failing.

THE ULTIMATE CLIENT

Thankfully, after two months of nothing, a series of unlikely events turned everything around for the corporate side of our business. It began when the usually silent phone on my desk rang. I recognized the voice on the other end immediately: Sue McFarland, Andy Grove's executive assistant. "We have a problem," she said. "I contacted Travel

Planners to arrange a trip for Andy, and they completely dropped the ball." Apparently, Andy, the notorious perfectionist, had become furious, raging, "I can't believe Maryles made a stupid mistake like that!"

Sue had replied, "It wasn't Maryles. She's not there anymore." At that point, as Sue related it, Andy panicked, certain that his reservations would be screwed up from there on out. When he calmed down, he told Sue, "Go find Maryles."

Those were the magic words. It took some effort on Sue's part, but now she was on the line, saying, "Andy wants you to handle this department." In other words: executive row at the firm recognized as "the world's most important company." How could it get any better than that? My prayers had been answered.

There was only one problem, and I decided to deal with it honestly: "That's really good," I told Sue, "but we don't have the money. We have to pay upfront for your tickets on a weekly basis, and we bill you monthly. We just don't have the cash."

Sue caught her breath. I'm sure she didn't want to break that news to Andy. "Let me see what I can do," she said and hung up. A few hours later, she called again: she was authorized by Intel Purchasing to give me a check for $20,000 in advance for services. When I drew that account down, Intel would replenish it.

Receiving that first check was a major accomplishment for us. It may as well have said, "You have arrived!" across it. Lee and I joked that we didn't want to cash it; we wanted to frame it. Of course, we needed the money in our account. Looking back, that check represented my very first management fee—a technique that would prove useful in the years to come.

I'm not sure whether all my sales calls were finally starting to pay off, or whether the Intel contract news had gotten out, legitimating our new business, but within a matter of days, I landed my second account, a disk drive company: Shugart Associates. I knew the founder, Al Shugart, from his Memorex days. He was an affable, laid-back guy who liked nothing more than going fishing and hitting a bar afterward. Even after he became a billionaire, Al never lost his common touch—or his eccentricity. That first trait changed my life; the second made him one of my favorite people.

Al wanted me to handle Shugart Associates travel, but I cautioned him, as I had Sue at Intel, about my lack of operating capital. True to character, he made a cash-on-delivery arrangement with us, which enabled us to manage cash flow in those early days. If Andy Grove made our agency legitimate, Al Shugart made us viable.

During this start-up period, I learned a great truth of Silicon Valley, one that holds, if to a lesser degree, even today. As Valley historian Michael S. Malone has written, "Silicon Valley is a large small town: Everybody in it has worked for, with, or against everyone else." That truth brought me my next big client.

In the family tree of modern Silicon Valley, Fairchild Semiconductor was the trunk from which all branches grew. It had been founded by the Traitorous Eight, defectors from Shockley Semiconductor Company. Of the eight, three of them were Robert Noyce, Gordon Moore—now-legendary figures, and Andy Grove's bosses at Intel—and Eugene Kleiner. Kleiner had procured the investment money that started Fairchild, and in the years since, while his fellow "Traitors" had gone on to found semiconductor companies, Kleiner had moved into funding those companies, cofounding Kleiner Perkins, a venture capital firm.

Through the Valley's unofficial network, Kleiner Perkins learned about Travel Experience, and I soon found myself in Eugene Kleiner's office, making my pitch.

He was a courtly, deeply kind gentleman who retained his Austrian accent his entire life. A Jew, he had escaped the Nazis and come to America to train as an industrial engineer. He married late, to his beloved Rose, whose pictures I saw strewn around his office. With his formal manners, he treated me with such respect, and by the end of our first meeting, he personally hired me to handle all Kleiner Perkins'—and his own—travel needs.

Over the years, I would watch Kleiner Perkins become a world-renowned venture capital firm, backing companies like Amazon, Twitter, Snap, Genentech, and Square, among many others. But Eugene Kleiner never changed. He remained a humble and deeply contented man. When I arranged the rare trip for Rose and him, he was always so polite and concerned he might be taking up too much of my time—of course, he never did. Eugene and Rose remained married for nearly fifty years, until her death. In their later years, they would dedicate themselves to philanthropy. Thousands of young Silicon Valleyites were born in the Eugene and Rose Kleiner maternity wing of El Camino Hospital.

As for Travel Experience—well, being a contractor to the most important venture capital firm in the tech world not only raised our profile even further but also gave us access to all of the hot new start-ups in which KP was investing. After all, venture capitalists did not only fund start-ups, they steered these companies to the best business partners—bankers, real estate brokers, legal counsel, marketing firms, and travel agencies. Now we were well positioned to become the go-to corporate travel agency for Silicon Valley.

With each new client, I grew more confident that Lee and I had made the right decision, stepping out on our own. As with thousands of other Silicon Valley start-ups, the odds against our success were long, but the winds were beginning to blow in our direction. It looked like smooth sailing from here on.

That's when I discovered that I was pregnant.

A WELCOME SURPRISE

"Maryles, what's going on with your boobs?"

I was standing with a friend at the precipice of a black diamond ski run, waiting for the rest of our party to unload from the chairlift.

"What?" I asked.

"Look at your boobs! They're huge! Are you pregnant?" my friend asked.

I looked down. Actually, I had noticed that my shirt was a little snug when I pulled it on that morning, but I hadn't thought much of it. Pregnant? Not possible. MarDell and I had tried for years. I'd had two miscarriages, after which my doctor had told me that it was unlikely that I would ever carry a baby to term. We'd been married eleven years now, and I had accepted that I would never be a mother. But come to think of it, I hadn't gotten my period for a while. Could I be?

I shrugged at my friend. "I don't think so," I said, then I eyed the steep slope ahead of me, mentally mapping the safest route through the moguls.

A few days later, a pregnancy test confirmed it. At the busiest and most critical time in my career to date, I was going to have a baby. It wasn't great timing for MarDell, either. He had just started a real estate development company, and they were preparing to launch their first big project, a new office building in Downtown San Jose. We had no idea how we were going to pull all this off, but we were both ecstatic about this unexpected news, while apprehensive about my body's ability to carry a baby to term. Like every other adventure we had leapt into, we would meet this one together.

Ever the researcher, MarDell jumped into reading all the pregnancy and baby care books. He signed us up for birth classes, at which he diligently practiced the breathing rituals while I wondered how long I was going to have to lie on the floor pretending to be in labor when I could be catching up on paperwork at the office. This isn't to say I wasn't interested in learning, but as I saw it, childbirth wouldn't be happening for months, while Travel Experience was growing faster than the baby in my belly—faster than I could keep up with.

In desperation, we hired our first employee, my cousin Patsy. In truth, Patsy had no business experience. In fact, she had never worked a day in her life. But she had two qualities we needed: we could afford her, and I trusted her, at least to perform tasks that didn't require a lot of training.

Patsy's first assignment was to drive up to San Francisco to pick up a visa and a passport for one of our corporate clients. This was a new service I had put into place to expand our portfolio of offerings for our customers. Unfortunately, Patsy had never driven in San Francisco before—a stressful activity for experienced drivers, and a nightmare for my cousin. When she finally returned to the office, she announced, "I resign; I can't do this."

But at this point, we couldn't lose her. So, I gave her a different assignment: she was to visit every parking lot of every business park in the Valley and keep a record of how many cars were in each one. If she noticed a full parking lot in front of a company that wasn't our client, she was to go into the lobby and find out from the receptionist if they had a travel agent, and if yes, who it was. That way, we were able to identify our competition and target which companies we might scoop up immediately. That was the sum of our business intelligence operation, and my cousin was my first sales and marketing professional. She enjoyed the work—anything not to have to drive into San Francisco again.

As for the rest of it—on the corporate side of our business, I was swamped even before I found out I was pregnant. Lee couldn't step in because she was unfamiliar with the nuances of serving corporate clients, and she was too busy with her vacation clients to learn. So, I was left dealing with a demanding client list, a steady stream of new customers, and a phone that seemed to never stop ringing. Not bad problems to have, of course, but in order to keep pace, we were going to need two things: more travel agents and more space.

So, by the time I was six months pregnant, we doubled the size of the Travel Experience team and orchestrated a move to a larger office, on Arques in Sunnyvale, where our two Repo Depot desks were joined by four more, where we had enough wall space to accommodate colorful world maps, and where I hung the painting that I had purchased for forty dollars in a place where everyone could enjoy it. Oh, and the ferns came with us, too. At our grand reopening, I met Andy Grove in person for the first time, and I learned that this notoriously exacting, demanding client was also kind enough to show up and celebrate the professional milestone of a contractor who had served him—without error—for years.

I loved the buzz of our new office—our six desks side by side in the main room, the phones' near-constant ringing, the excitement of training new agents to provide our particular brand of customer care while also showing those agents a respect they seldom had seen in the industry. I was activating the items on that mental list of "things I will do differently if I ever have an agency of my own"—and it felt great.

Amid this buzz, I worked all through my pregnancy, until two days before I went into labor.

MOTHERHOOD

MarDell and I welcomed a little boy on September 6, 1975. We named him Marc Jonas. I took a month off work to get to know this sweet baby, to learn the ropes of early motherhood, and to consider how I would balance these two roles of mine, mother and entrepreneur.

First, let me say a little something about adjusting to motherhood: I knew absolutely nothing about taking care of a baby. Nothing. I had never changed a diaper, fed a baby, comforted a fussy newborn, or rocked a baby to sleep. I did not know any lullabies, nursery rhymes, or baby games. Remember, my mother had household staff to help her care for and entertain us in our youngest years. Babysitting was nowhere in my work history. There was never a time when my mother had laid a younger sibling in my lap and said, "Keep an eye on him while I run an errand."

Luckily, MarDell's research made up for my lack of experience. He taught me how to change a diaper—and those were cloth diapers, held on with safety pins that felt anything but safe when I was stabbing them into fabric so close to Marc's tiny belly. MarDell taught me how to hold, feed, burp, and soothe our son. Most importantly, unlike many fathers at that time, he did not assume taking care of Marc was my job alone. We were in this as a team.

Meanwhile, as those blurry newborn days blended one into the next, I found myself thinking about work—and my future—from a new perspective.

It occurred to me that Lee and I had made a good team, inspiring and supporting each other, as we stepped out on our own. As Travel Experience had expanded, though, I had noticed a difference between us. As I saw it, we had a window of opportunity in this high-energy tech world, and we needed to take full advantage of it, grabbing up as many clients as we could, start-ups and established companies alike. I didn't care if that meant taking risks; I wanted to go for it. Lee was not so inclined. She worried that the start-up accounts might not make it, and we would lose any money we spent up front to secure their travel arrangements when they inevitably closed up shop. I wanted to ride the wave, but I did not want to take Lee down if we failed. Even more, I wanted the agency to become a major player, which would require investing our profits back into the firm to finance that growth. Lee did not share that dream, nor was she interested in reinvesting her earnings. Ultimately, if I wanted to keep flying upward, I would need to do it on my own.

When I returned to work, I offered Lee a generous cash buyout, and she took it. It was an amicable parting. Lee kept the Travel Experience name and found an office in Mountain View. I kept the office on Arques and set to rearranging the furniture. I was ready to get back to work, but I was not nearly ready to leave Marc in someone else's care, so with the blessing and enthusiasm of the team, we turned our lunchroom into a nursery, complete with a crib, diaper-changing table, rocking chair, toys, books, and *Sesame Street* characters adorning the walls. It might have been the first corporate on-site childcare facility in Silicon Valley.

Now only one thing was missing: a company name. Our team suggested we call the company Casto Travel. I hesitated, knowing the responsibility that lies in having your name on the door. Growing up in my family, I learned that your name is your honor, and your honor is your name. My father took this to heart and impressed it upon all his children. If I agreed to name the company Casto Travel, I wasn't putting just my name out there, but MarDell's and Marc's, too. The honor of their name would be not only in my hands but in the hands of all current and future employees. I needed to know we would all commit to live up to it ourselves, and to train any future associates to do the same. The team wholeheartedly agreed—they believed in our unique brand of service, they loved our positive work environment, and they would uphold what they came to call our "CastoWay."

SOLO

As 1976 began, I found myself exactly where I was destined to be: a solo entrepreneur, running a fast-growing business, responsible for my own fate—and the fates of my growing team. Like any high-risk stunt, it was both thrilling and frightening. I'd never been so energized.

Our Sunnyvale office was right in the heart of the Valley's industrial district. Aside from the Casto Travel sign out front, it was indistinguishable from all the other concrete tilt-up buildings in the area—and that's the way I liked it. I wanted Silicon Valley companies to look at us as one of them.

One of our neighbors was another start-up, Devcon. At the time, it was a small construction company with a vision for broad expansion. But you could already tell they were destined for much bigger things. The leaders behind the expansion, Jim Blair, Larry Russel, and Gary Filizetti, were terrific guys. I recognized in them the same entrepreneurial fire I felt in myself. They, too, were laboring to make their place. Though we worked in vastly different fields, we were compatriots, fighting the good fight for our two companies, side by side. It was comforting to know that others were going through what I was, the ups and downs, the good times and bad. In the end, their dreams came true, too: Devcon became and remains the largest general contractor in Silicon Valley, with their signs posted on construction sites across the Valley and tens of millions of square feet of office space bearing their stamp. I couldn't be happier for them.

If on the outside Casto Travel was indistinguishable from our tech neighbors, things were much different inside our building. Not only did the décor in our "lunchroom" look more preschool classroom than Fortune 500, but Marc let everyone know he was in residence when he was hungry, which seemed to happen every two hours.

It was rare in those days to see a baby in a corporate office—it probably still is—but most clients were understanding. They knew that I was a first-time mom, with all the anxieties that come with that. I can't tell you how many phone calls I took from captains of industry as I bounced Marc on my lap.

During this period, I learned, to my eternal gratitude, about the sisterhood of mothers. With an office full of women and an army of executive secretaries on our client list, I received endless support from mothers who had been there and done that. They gave me tips for changing Marc's clothes without traumatizing either of us, they taught me nursery rhymes and tricks for avoiding diaper rash. Most importantly, they entertained Marc when I absolutely needed to focus on my work.

One of our new clients was Signetics, the giant semiconductor company headquartered just around the corner from our office. My contact there was Connie Frey, secretary to CEO Chuck Harwood. Regularly she would walk over during her lunch break and play with Marc so I could rush out and meet clients face to face. Those clients must have wondered why I always scheduled meetings at lunchtime.

As Marc grew older, he needed more space to move around and play. One of our agents mentioned that her grandmother, who lived close by, would be willing to babysit. She was an elderly woman who spoke mostly Spanish, but coming from a multilingual household, I didn't care that her English wasn't too good, I cared that her maternal love was for the ages. With her support, we fell into a new routine. From the time Marc woke up until ten a.m., my time belonged to him. He had my full attention, and I wouldn't allow myself to be rushed. Then we packed up, and on the way to the office, I handed him off into his babysitter's loving arms. Once I arrived at the office, I switched roles from Mom to Entrepreneur. I was 100 percent dedicated to Casto Travel until 5:30 p.m., when, no matter what I was doing, I would leave the office, shed my Business Self, pick up my Mom Self, and retrieve Marc from the babysitter.

By compartmentalizing work and parenting, I made sure I could be fully present with each in their turn. I didn't sneak out to see Marc during my workday—though God knows I wanted to—and I didn't answer work calls when I was with Marc. Instead, I depended on my staff to deal with anything that came up, trusting they knew how to step in for me. Setting those boundaries likely compromised Casto Travel's growth for a couple years, but I never regretted it.

Of course, this plan worked because I had wonderful support from both Marc's caretaker and the Casto team during business hours, and from MarDell at home. I can say with absolute certainty that if it hadn't been for them, I might have gone crazy.

Running a start-up and being a mother isn't for the faint of heart. Especially in Silicon Valley, where growth was so fast-paced, demands were so high, and everything had to happen *now*. I was making sales presentations, attending travel seminars, and implementing new accounts while also booking reservations for CEOs who wanted only me to handle their travel. Combine that with the broken sleep all mothers know, and I was a walking zombie, constantly nagged by the feeling that I might have missed an important detail.

Of course, with so much up in the air, even the most skilled juggler is going to drop a ball eventually. For me, that ball was a reservation for a client we really needed to impress: Don Massaro, a new CEO who had just taken the helm of Shugart Associates. Someone had booked the wrong hotel for him, and by the time the mistake was discovered, the right hotel was sold out. I was mortified. We had built this company on a reputation for perfect reliability and impeccable service, and my name was on the door. That's when, for the first time since Casto Travel had begun our high-speed ascent, I slammed the brakes.

I called the entire staff together and told them, "You know what? We need to stop, now, because what we're doing is crap. We're making mistakes. We're not checking our work. We've grown sloppy. We are going to clean up this mess, and then we're going to stop taking any new clients until we figure out if our processes are working right and if we have the right people in the right seats. We need to refocus on the level of service that we've always promised our customers. Until we get those things right, we don't deserve to be in business."

Rather than feeling chastised, the staff was relieved. They knew things were falling apart. They knew we weren't living up to the standards we had set. I also think they knew, as I did in my heart, that my complaints were as much directed at myself as at them. I had learned another abiding truth.

Lesson: Runaway success can be just as fraught as failure.

CHAPTER 4

RECESSION AND RENAISSANCE

In our first year doing business as Casto Travel, we brought in $500,000 in sales. By the end of our second year, we hit the million-dollar mark, and the Casto team grew to nine employees. By the early 1980s, we had fine-tuned our operations, and our challenge was no longer finding new accounts but welcoming the steady stream of clients who were now finding us, serving them with our signature hospitality and meticulous customer care. Companies that had been little start-ups a few years prior were now racing toward one billion dollars in sales—with commensurate needs for travel management. We were hiring people left and right, just to keep up with demand. It seemed like nothing could stop us.

A NEW HIRE

One of those new hires happened to be my father, who, after visiting us regularly since my mother's death, had decided to make the United States—and more specifically, MarDell's and my house—his permanent home. Now, in addition to Mom, Wife, and Businessperson, I had another role to play: Daughter. I began to envision my life as one of those beautiful Chinese apothecary cabinets, with all the little drawers—I had a drawer for each area of my life, and I became adept at opening and closing them at will.

By the time Marc started school, MarDell was fully engaged in his real estate development company, and my father—never one to rest idle—needed something to do. So, I set him up in Casto Travel's ticketing department, assembling tickets and tucking them into travel folders. It was elementary work for someone with his life experience, but he enjoyed the comradery of the team, and I enjoyed watching the father I had caught a glimpse of in Spain emerge into his full glory here—quick with a joke, always up for a prank, a full participant in the Casto Travel fun, from crazy hat day to costume contests. No one called him "Mr. Vallejo" at work. Never "Rafael." To all of us, he was "Daddy."

This wasn't just a lark for him, though. He took his work seriously, adhering to the "CastoWay," which took detail orientation to a new level, down to the direction we stapled our tickets—with the prongs gripping the front of the ticket, not the back. This "backward" staple could seem an insignificant detail—even a mistake—unless you consider where business travelers tended to carry their travel documents: in their breast pockets, where a sharp staple could snag a suit coat or dress shirt. Anyway, my father was such a decisive, experienced leader that he quickly took command of the whole ticketing department and built his own loyal following.

As much as I loved having my father at work with me, his presence there challenged my compartmentalization strategy. At home, I could be Daughter, but I needed my father to understand that when I walked through the office door, I became a different person. I was no longer a child who needed guidance; I was the captain of the Casto ship, responsible for all passengers on board. Over time, he came to respect my abilities in the office and the role I played there, and at home, we adhered to a strict policy: no talking about work. Home was for family meals, dominoes, helping Marc with his homework, and cheering so loudly at his school performances and ball games that he was too embarrassed to look in our direction.

SURPRISE

As Casto Travel's sales ticked upward, United Airlines took notice. Just as we did with our clients, the airline put great effort into developing a positive relationship with us—to an extent that surprised me, literally.

For my fortieth birthday, MarDell, six-year-old Marc, and I planned a trip to Hawaii. I was excited to go, but I'll admit, I was feeling a little nervous about leaving my father behind in California. Before we took off, I tried to call him from the airport, but he didn't answer, which was unusual. *I'll call him when we reach the hotel,* I told myself. *I'm sure he's fine.*

On the flight, I struck up a conversation with the governor of Hawaii, who happened to be sitting nearby. I told him where we'd be staying—the Kahala Hotel—and I asked what he knew about the restaurant there. He told me it was wonderful. So, I started dreaming about the fantastic meal my family would have that night.

Well, once we settled in at the Hilton, both of my plans fell through. First, my father didn't answer my call. Then MarDell—for some inexplicable reason—refused to go to dinner downstairs.

"I don't want to go down there," he said. "We won't get a table."

I said, "MarDell, I talked to the maître d' on our way in. He said they can take us tonight."

"No, no," he said. "I want to go to the Outrigger."

"All the way to Waikiki?" I argued. "Why would we go there?" I was really getting a bit upset—I mean, it was my birthday celebration, after all.

MarDell was adamant, so the three of us piled back into the car, and I grumbled all the way to the restaurant, when I wasn't busy wondering about my father, that is. By the time we arrived, I was hungry enough not to care where my food came from, but it looked like we'd have to wait, judging by the long line outside the restaurant. So, there I was, all dressed up for my birthday, starving, walking toward the back of the line, when all of the sudden, a waiter comes out and says, "Casto party?"

I thought, *Wow! Okay. Now we're getting somewhere.*

MarDell, Marc, and I followed the waiter inside the restaurant, across the dining room, and into a private room, where I finally understood why MarDell had insisted: United Airlines had flown the entire Casto Travel team, including my dad, to Waikiki to celebrate my fortieth birthday. I couldn't believe it—not only that United would do something so generous, but that my work family would disrupt their own lives to fly three thousand miles and celebrate mine. I was speechless.

NEW DIRECTIONS

By the early 1980s, I had been around Silicon Valley long enough to know that it regularly—about every four years—suffered economic downturns to match its booms. In the back of my mind, I knew a crash might happen again one day, but to date, Casto Travel had really only known good times. Besides, I figured I'd see warning signs ahead of a pending crash so I'd have plenty of time to prepare. Like a swimmer in the movie *Jaws*, I couldn't hear the soundtrack foreshadowing doom; I was too busy paddling toward the next big wave.

In 1983, Casto Travel's revenues reached approximately $30 million—a remarkable growth curve given where we had started. Being my usual self, rather than resting on this peak, I considered it a plateau and continued trekking forward, expanding vertically by offering new services and horizontally by seeking new territory outside the Valley. Looking back, had we taken a conservative approach and stuck to our core competence (booking airline tickets and hotel reservations) and our existing market (Silicon Valley), Casto Travel might have disappeared in the face of what was to come. Instead, unknowingly, we positioned ourselves perfectly to survive.

In working with the Valley's executives, it had become apparent to me that beyond business trips, in their private travels, our clients wanted not only airline, hotel, and car reservations but all of the other experiences and amenities that come with high-end vacations—tickets to the theater or sporting events, tables at the exclusive restaurants, and unique tours planned just for them. So, Casto Travel set about providing full-service travel assistance, a move that, I now understand, opened the door for what had been strictly professional relationships with Silicon Valley icons to become deeply personal friendships. More on that later.

Around the same time, our corporate clients began to come to us with requests for assistance in planning off-site group events, which sparked a game-changing realization: meeting planning and employee incentive programs were an untapped market. Peter Carter was one of the first to ask us to create a special package for its top employees. The Casto Team organized a full-blown Agatha Christie experience on the Orient Express, from London to Venice. Eighty-five employees went, all of them in period costumes, enjoying surprise events along the way. Pulling this off was a big challenge for our team, but we had such fun dreaming up and executing every detail. Once word got out about this new service, we were inundated with similar requests.

The Orient Express trip inspired a new idea to pitch to our clients: Why not offer a more customizable incentive program to reward top performers, celebrate employee milestones, and incentivize salespeople? Instead of planning a group excursion, which may or may not suit an employee's tastes, schedule, or lifestyle, this program allowed client companies to issue beautiful, custom-printed "travel awards"—$5,000, $10,000, $25,000—so recipients could work with Casto Travel to build personalized travel experiences they would never forget.

Booking those award trips proved to be a fair amount of work, but employees loved them, using them in any number of ways—taking cruises with their families, checking boxes on their bucket lists, or upgrading their business trips to first-class flights and five-star hotels. An impressive number of companies took us up on this offer, further expanding our business and strengthening our bonds with our clients.

Lesson: Don't give your customers the service you want to provide but the service they want to receive.

It was the CastoWay to learn everything we could about our clients so we could not only fulfill their expectations, not only anticipate their needs, but also determine what they would want when they saw it. Further, we believed we were responsible for our clients' travel experiences from the moment they left their front doors until they returned home. So, we stayed available throughout their trips, ready to smooth out any unanticipated bumps along the way. As a result, our travelers felt seen, heard, understood, cared for, and protected—key components of long-term relationships, in business and beyond.

BRANCHING OUT

My horizontal move during this period was to actively reduce my dependence upon Silicon Valley. No matter how different computer chips looked from personal computers, or software looked from communications hardware, I knew enough about tech business to understand that these companies moved up and down together. Falling orders in one sector—especially chips—would soon be reflected in all the others. To guard against this insecurity, we needed to stretch beyond the Valley into industries that had their own, different, cycles.

San Francisco seemed a natural choice, both because it was only forty miles away and because the Casto team was already running up there regularly to meet customers at San Francisco Airport or obtain passports and visas. Moreover, back then, the city had not yet become the tech business enclave it is today. Rather, it was a hub for professional service providers—banking, investment, legal, advertising—for the Valley and far beyond. It was also home to potential non-tech clients, like Levi's, Wells Fargo, and government offices. Not to mention, my ambitious nature had me gunning to become a big-time player in that famous city to the north.

Once I set my mind to something, I move fast, so in a blink, I had signed a lease on a storefront office on Taylor Street, and I set about redecorating it. Gone were our Repo Depot days. This office had plush furniture, original art on the walls, and a wonderfully soothing color scheme. I wanted it to look impressive for clients who visited, yes, but I also wanted to create a beautiful location for the Casto Team to work, so I spared no detail.

One of those details gained Casto Travel some unexpected attention. United Airlines had decided to standardize their reservation terminals, requiring the entire global United system, including travel agents, to use the same branded terminals. Well, the terminals, painted "United blue," clashed with my new office design, so I had them repainted a lovely salmon orange. It never occurred to me to ask permission. Word of our salmon terminals got out, United officials informed me of my branding crime, and they insisted I repaint the equipment in the proper shade of blue. I refused. Luckily, by that point, we were one of United's top-performing agencies and they didn't want to lose us, so they gave up the fight, but not before it became a story in the travel industry's trade magazines.

In fact, we would keep our salmon terminals for years, until United itself replaced all the blue terminals with off-white. Then we relented, but only because the new color fit with our décor.

Lesson: Don't acquiesce to arbitrary rules. Make the right choice for you.

Meanwhile, our San Francisco operations took off quickly, and just as quickly, I realized I had made a horrible mistake. In my search for an office, I had ignored the three most important qualities in real estate: location, location, location. I thought it would be fun to be adjacent to Union Square, with its iconic Saint Francis Hotel, nearby cable car line, and constant buzz of shoppers and tourists. Situated across the street from the Israeli embassy, however, the only buzz we heard came from political protests. Not to mention our clients were not the only people who appreciated our nicely appointed lobby—it wasn't unusual to find a homeless person, desperate for a comfortable place to lie down, wandering through the office or sleeping on our couch.

What was I thinking? We weren't a vacation agency; we were a corporate agency. We didn't belong in a tourist trap; we needed to be in the Financial District. So, we packed up our beautiful décor and moved to a business suite on Montgomery Street.

That mistake opened my eyes to something: I had always been a bit impulsive, doing what felt right in the moment—from turning a nun's garbage-can punishment into a school-wide party, to trusting love to bridge the gap between my world and MarDell's, to quitting Travel Partners with little more than a dream to carry me forward. For the most part, my giant leaps had served me well. But now, this wasn't a solo flight. The plane was full of employees who trusted me, and I needed to calibrate my risks, for us all. Perhaps my elementary school teachers would be happy to hear I finally understood, viscerally, why it's important to complete all—or at least most—of the steps, rather than jumping from one to ten.

Despite my location mistake, before long, we grew our roster of San Francisco clients, adding World Savings, Union Bank, Robertson Stephens investment, and, reluctantly, Government Services Administration. I say "reluctantly" because, though it was a huge account, it was also government bureaucracy, with all the paperwork and late payments that entailed.

Simultaneously, we continued our growth in the Valley, opening an office in Palo Alto, alongside mature companies like Hewlett-Packard and Varian, and closer to my real targets: Stanford University and the many venture capital firms on Sand Hill Road. I had already landed a couple of them—now I wanted to capture the rest.

At this point, I was feeling pretty confident. The crowning moment came when I drove up to our new Palo Alto office on California Street. Something about that big green awning over the front door, emblazoned with giant letters reading "Casto Travel"—the moment I saw it, I thought, *That's it. We've made it.*

Then the recession hit.

THREAT RESPONSE

The 1984 recession was the worst that Silicon Valley had experienced to date. Naively, Valleyites behaved as though we were inoculated against economic downturns—our technology was too hot, our companies too smart, and our presence too strong in too many different markets for all of them to go down simultaneously. We were wrong on every count.

The US Army teaches its soldiers that, when they are ambushed, the worst thing they can do is to hunker down. Being defensive against an unseen enemy is usually fatal. Rather, the best strategy is to figure out where the bullets are coming from and charge forward, taking the offensive. In business, economic downturns are like ambushes. They are usually all but unexpected, they often produce panic, and one of the worst things you can do is to go into a defensive crouch.

Lesson: An economic downturn—if you charge right at it—can be the best possible opportunity.

For a business owner, going on the offensive at a time like this isn't easy. For one thing, it most likely will require austerity measures, layoffs, or even office closures. Furthermore, cautious senior staff and advisers are likely to resist any bold moves you might want to make. Finally, you will spend a lot of sleepless nights wondering if you are doing the right thing. That said, if you look at the histories of the greatest companies, many of them catapulted to new heights by taking great risks during hard times. Doing so, they gained a head start when business turned upward, capturing market share so quickly their competitors couldn't catch up.

I was hardly an expert on business theory in those days, but I had an intuitive sense that now was the moment to make my move. However, this time, before leaping, I calculated my risk. Were we stable enough to push forward? Thanks to our geographic expansion, our recently added services, and our client diversification, I believed we were. We had some money in the bank, and our non-tech clients hadn't fallen into the recession as quickly as our tech clients had.

But then the travel industry was hit by a second economic blow.

In 1984, a new government regulation reduced travel agent commissions from 10 percent for all purchases over $100 to just 8 percent—a seemingly small percentage shift for a single transaction that stretched into a wide chasm at scale. Over the course of the rest of the decade, that rate would continue to drop until it reached zero.

As you can imagine, this devastated travel agencies that made most of their profit off those commissions, driving thousands of agencies to shut their doors, scramble to find buyers, or consolidate, if they could. It was a buyer's market, and thanks to a serendipitous turn of events, Casto Travel was ready to shop.

What was the turn? Ahead of the commission cut, I had already begun to shift my business model from commissions to management fees. Remember that $20,000 check that Intel cut for Travel Experience, giving us the cash cushion we needed to handle the account? Well, when the economy turned, and our impacted clients began delaying payments, once again, I needed to smooth out cash flow. Why not ask some of my key accounts, with whom I had long-term relationships, to switch over to a management fee model as well?

As far as I know, nobody in the travel industry had ever tried such a thing. But thanks to the unique relationships I had built with Silicon Valley leaders, I felt comfortable calling CEOs directly and pitching my plan. After all, we had built our companies side by side, Casto Travel had served them well, they depended on us both professionally and personally, and I think many of them had a small emotional stake in our success. For all of those reasons, they had no objections to paying us a monthly fee rather than dealing with individual transactions.

I ramped up this transformation in our pricing model when the first commission cut was announced. By the time commissions disappeared entirely, most of our accounts had moved to our fee model—and those that hadn't done so accepted a fee based on service rendered. That, as much as anything we did, saved us.

Lesson: Pricing can be your most valuable competitive tool.

With these measures keeping Casto relatively stable, beginning in 1984, we went into full acquisition mode for two years, buying up agencies, most of them in bad financial straits, for a fraction of their value. Every one of these acquisitions was a tough decision, because Casto Travel wasn't much better off, but it was not enough for me to survive the economic downturn; I wanted to leverage it to grow. To me, the risks were well worth the potential reward.

I made one more important move during this difficult period. Not convinced that we could maintain all of our existing clients, who themselves were suffering losses and layoffs, I decided to add a new branch to the business. This, too, was an anxiety-producing decision, but I felt we had no choice: nobody knew how long this recession might last, nor if we had hit bottom yet.

So, since any unwritten agreement I might have had with my old partner had long since expired, we announced that Casto Travel was going into the vacation business. After all, it wasn't like we didn't understand that world: with all of those employee award plans we had designed, and all the personal trips we had planned for our executive clients, we'd already stuck our toes in that water.

I even had a target customer base. Using my new Palo Alto office, I went after professors at Stanford, who weren't suffering from the recession, and people in the nearby wealthy enclaves of Woodside and Los Altos Hills, whose fortunes—and lifestyles—had not changed.

While the other initiatives kept Casto Travel above water, the vacation income helped finance our acquisition strategy, and gave us a whole new cohort of loyal clients.

During those few years, I felt like the cat in the poster from that era—dangling from a tree branch, front claws desperately gripping the bark, above the caption "Hang in there!" We were never *not* in trouble, never free of losing everything, always low on cash. We were inundated with so many scares, challenges, and near misses that as soon as we solved one, two more were waiting in the wings. But here's the upside of being a person who can't sit still: I loved the action. Where others in my industry cowered, I developed the attitude that if Casto Travel was going to go down, we would do so fighting to the last.

I didn't spend a lot of time thinking about failure, though. In my mind, we had to succeed. There were no other options. We had to keep moving. We had to keep growing. Though I carried a deep sense of responsibility for the livelihoods of my team, I wasn't worried for myself. I was still young—just forty-five years old. My husband had a job. My son understood the crazy, up-and-down world of start-ups. I had built this company from the ground up, and I could do it again. Even if Casto Travel fell from these heights, my family would not suffer mightily, and I knew I would bounce all the way back.

Lesson: An entrepreneur is willing to bet it all for the company.

Happily, I didn't have to take that ultimate test. Within months of opening the Palo Alto office, we landed the $10 million Syntex account. Then Varian Associates. Then Electromagnetic Systems Laboratory (ESL). To be closer to these huge companies, we moved our office right into the middle of the famous Stanford Industrial Park, just blocks from mighty Hewlett-Packard. We never did get the HP account, but what really mattered to me about that company was the example it set. I wanted to be the HP of the travel world—quality products, trustworthiness, and a great place to work. I like to think that I got as close as anyone in my industry.

A VERY PUBLIC RECOVERY

Though at the time it seemed like forever, the 1984 downturn was already ending by 1986. As the Silicon Valley economy improved, and as both companies and individuals began to feel prosperity's return, at Casto Travel, we reaped the payoff for our hard work and high-risk investments. By 1988, our sales revenue reached $50 million, and our team had grown to thirty employees.

Marc was now a teenager, applying to high schools and quickly becoming his dad's favorite co-adventurer. MarDell, I see in hindsight, was beginning to chafe at the ropes tying us to Silicon Valley. Ever in search of new experiences, he was contemplating his next move. I was too caught up managing the compartments of my life to notice.

Women in my generation were facing a conundrum. We were proving that, yes, we could make our place in business, but we were still expected to—and many of us expected ourselves to—fulfill traditional roles at home. MarDell was different from many men—he was a hands-on dad from the beginning, he wholeheartedly supported my career, and he was the one who taught me how to cook and take care of a house, but after I learned, though MarDell helped out, I felt the housework was my responsibility. My father reinforced that idea. Remember, he lived with us, and as much as he embraced his daughter's entrepreneurial pursuits, he was not shy about telling me when he believed I was failing in my duties as a homemaker. What did that look like? After a long day's work, my father expected me to come home and cook dinner for everyone. Even if I had an evening meeting or event, I'd come home and find my father—and later, when my brother Tony moved in with us, him, too—not just waiting for me to cook dinner but complaining about the wait. Sometimes I'd think, *Why are you all waiting for me? Go ahead and get started on your own.*

When I look back on it now, it seems crazy. My father, my brother, and I all worked at the same office all day—why did only one of us have a job when we got home? But that's what can happen when a household spans generations and cultures—opinions bang into each other, contradictions coexist, and you do your best to navigate them. My father and brother may have moved to the United States, but their expectations of me came directly from the Philippines.

Come to think of it, so did mine. I wanted to be good at all my roles—Businesswoman, Mother, Daughter, Sister, Wife. So, when I got home, it was like an automatic switch: I started cooking a homemade sit-down meal. It never occurred to me to take a shortcut—pick up takeout or grab something out of the freezer—or to insist on a redivision of labor in the house. Cooking was my way of loving my family, and meals were our time to connect. In Marc's memories, we're always in the kitchen. From the time that he was a little boy, I would put him in his seat, and I would be at the counter, and I'd be cooking and singing and talking. Even today, Marc loves being in the kitchen, and that makes me so happy.

Meanwhile, at the office, I was working as hard as ever. When your company is going well, you work hard and all but pray for a slowdown so you can relax. Then the slowdown comes, and you need to scramble more than ever to keep the company afloat. The bottom line: you *never* get to slow down. Besides, anytime Casto Travel reached a safe holding ground, I immediately started looking for the next challenge. That's just what I do.

At that point, many of our biggest competitors had fallen prey to the recession and commission regulations. Others were now part of the Casto Travel family. We were looking at the clearest competitive landscape we had ever experienced. How would we take advantage of this unique opportunity?

Lesson: How you come out of a recession is just as important as how you got through it.

Needless to say, we immediately notched up our staffing to meet increased demand without compromising the quality of our service. But that alone, I realized, wasn't enough. The challenge now was to consolidate our success, to find a way to raise Casto Travel's profile so that we didn't have to wait for word of mouth to spread our reputation. We needed to become a name that *everyone* knew in the region, whether they were our clients or not. We needed to become the agency everyone thought of first when they needed travel planning.

Once again, serendipity found me a solution.

Over the years, I had become increasingly involved in the social and cultural life of Silicon Valley. Having been so blessed by this town, I felt I needed to give something back. So, I had added yet another compartment to my Chinese cabinet: volunteer work. I began attending fundraisers, joining boards of nonprofits, and generally committing myself to improving life in my community. At one of these events, I met Brenna Bolger, who owned one of the most successful PR firms in San Jose. She was bright, ambitious, and endlessly energetic. One of the talents I most admired in her—and still do—was her ability to take a collection of facts, anecdotes, and historical events from a client and craft them into a concise, compelling story that would capture the imagination of the media and, by extension, the general public. At the time, Brenna's agency, PRxDigital, mostly served local hospitals, government agencies, nonprofits, and a few tech companies—but no travel agencies. In fact, I'm not sure a regional travel agency had ever hired a public relations firm. None that I encountered had. But it struck me that we had a story, too. That somewhere in the high-speed blur of Casto Travel's previous ten years—and my own unusual backstory— there must have been a powerful, entertaining story to be told. So, I hired Brenna and unleashed her to find it.

In the end, she not only found it but she sold that story to the world. Part of it was the appealing plot: *Entrepreneurial stewardess from the Philippines opens travel agency that has captured the loyalty of Silicon Valley's leading companies.* One newspaper described Casto Travel's service as combining "Asian hospitality and Yankee business sense." I loved that. This initial promotional success quickly led to one of the most memorable moments in my career.

To take advantage of this growing publicity, Brenna approached the San Jose *Mercury News*—one of the most influential newspapers in the country at the time—about doing a profile of me. It was a long shot. The best I could have hoped for was a small story in the Sunday business section. But then, magic happened.

A photographer from the *Merc*, working with Brenna, hatched an ambitious plan for a photo to lead the story: me, dressed exquisitely, standing in front of a typical office desk, staring at the camera lens—a pretty standard business pose, *except* the desk would be located in a field beside the runways of San Jose International Airport, and the photo timed just as a passenger jet took off behind me. It would be the kind of photograph *Fortune* magazine might run alongside a major profile. I loved the idea.

In the end, it took three hours to get the shot right. I had to stand there, looking professional and composed, inches away from a wind-swept asphalt runway, waiting between takeoffs, as rabbits hopped past in the field, and the photographer struggled to capture the right plane at exactly the right time. At one point, I later learned, a United Airlines captain called the tower, saying, "What the hell is going on out here? There's a woman on the runway standing at a desk."

In the end, the photograph was a sensation, winning the photographer numerous awards. Even today, more than thirty years later, people still remember it. That's why I put it on the cover of this book. It seems to capture who I was at the time—a maverick style, a willingness to take risks. And that plane taking off? My dreams.

Years later, I would approach San Jose Airport—now Norman Y. Mineta San Jose International Airport—to see if I could duplicate the photo on its anniversary. But Silicon Valley had changed too much—the airport was nearly three times the size it had been—and the world had become too dangerous. Security refused to let me through.

WINGING IT

Brenna's team helped me create another lasting image: the Casto Travel logo. I had only one request for the design: that they incorporate a bird in it somehow. On our stationery, business cards, office doors, ticket folders—I wanted our logo to represent the spirit of travel, the power of flight. On a more personal level, ever since I was a little girl, it has always been my dream to be a bird, to soar across the sky, dipping and looping at my whim. That was the impetus for my love of flying with my father, my career as a flight attendant, and founding Casto Travel. Even now, I'm convinced that when I die, I will come back as a bird.

The design they came up with included the spread wings of a bird embedded in the letter *A* in Casto. Every time I looked at it, the bird reminded me of who I was, and what propelled me forward.

SURVIVORS

Casto Travel closed out the 1980s on an upswing. In 1990, our sales revenue hit $65 million, we had three major offices, and ten on-site centers servicing companies like Conner Peripherals, Software Publishing Corporation, PepsiCo, and Lockheed. We would face more economic downturns and threats ahead, but we had learned from the first one. We would never be caught so unprepared again, and the tools and techniques we had used in the 1984 crash would serve us well in the future. For now, though, we could take advantage of the good times, working closely with some of the most memorable companies and individuals in business history.

CHAPTER 5

LEARNING FROM THE BEST

When Casto Travel launched in 1975, Silicon Valley was the primordial sea from which world-changing companies, technologies, and business cultures would emerge. While the Valley certainly maintains that reputation today, it's hard to describe those early years to people who did not live them. Our company grew up alongside Intel, Apple, Seagate, Kleiner Perkins, Syntex, and Cisco. Casto Travel worked closely with future icons like Andy Grove, Robert Noyce, Gordon Moore, Steve Jobs, Al Shugart, and Finis Conner. Though we were entrepreneurs in different fields, we shared experiences common to anyone laboring to lift a start-up off the ground. At the same time, because of the business I was in—providing seamless corporate and personal travel experiences—I developed deep relationships with these people. Despite the Valley's geographic sprawl and constant stream of newcomers, in many ways, it operated—and in some ways, still does operate—as a small community, where the same cast of characters attended dinner parties, ribbon-cutting ceremonies, IPO celebrations, and fundraising galas; where social, business, and family networks became inextricably intertwined; and where the air constantly buzzed with the energy of the next big idea.

Much has been said about the seemingly insurmountable barriers businesswomen have faced in the Valley and beyond, especially those of us who came up during the 1970s and 1980s: the closed doors, the dismissive attitudes, the abuses, the bro culture. God knows if the Me Too movement had surged back then, some of the Valley's most iconic names would mean nothing to us today. I don't need to say more about these challenges here. They still exist, and women continue to overcome them, with incredible intelligence, power, resilience, and creativity, every day.

Instead, I would like to talk about what worked for me as a woman entrepreneur, growing a company from one employee to as many as three hundred, from one office to fifteen, from a $1,500 capital investment to $200 million in yearly sales revenues at its peak—and keeping it afloat through the ups and downs of a notoriously volatile economy. Along the way, I'll share a few stories about that amazing cast of characters, the Silicon Valley luminaries, some of whom became not only my clients but my confidants, advisers, and lifelong friends.

THE FIRST CLIENT: INTEL

If my first business strategy was "never stop moving," my second was "learn as you go." When I started this journey, I knew very little about business. I knew the travel industry inside and out. I knew how to provide impeccable, highly personalized customer care, and how to coach employees to do the same. I also knew the kind of work environment I wanted to create—respectful, rewarding, and fun. The rest I had to learn along the way. So, I was constantly reading, observing, asking questions, and most of all listening to the people around me. In Silicon Valley, I had the opportunity to learn from the very best, beginning with my primary client, Intel.

Intel Corporation was founded in the late 1960s by former executives of Fairchild Semiconductor, including Robert Noyce and Gordon Moore, and later joined by Andy Grove. As Fairchild Semiconductor—once a giant in the Valley—crumbled, more than a hundred companies emerged from the wreckage, but Intel was the most successful, ranked in the early 2000s as the most valuable manufacturing company in the world.

Bob Noyce was a famously charismatic leader, and Gordon Moore—the namesake of Moore's law—was a scientific genius. But much of Intel's success can be attributed to Andy Grove, whose dynamic—and often terrifying—management style made Intel into a world leader. In that sense, Intel and Casto Travel had something in common—Andy's impossibly high expectations and inability to tolerate mistakes, which led him to become Casto Travel's first client and helped accelerate both companies' ascents above our competitors.

From the start, Intel stood out from its counterparts in Silicon Valley. Not only were the founders historic innovators—most famously inventing the microprocessor, a candidate for the product of the century—but their management philosophy was different as well. For example, consider just my point of contact with the company: executive travel. Unlike the other companies I worked with, Intel's top brass never traveled first class. They traveled coach. In one of my earliest interactions with Bob Noyce, I called him because I had purchased a $900 ticket for him to New York City, but then I found a $299 ticket available at a slightly less convenient time. Bob instantly changed his reservation, not because Intel was tight on cash but because waste is waste, even if it does buy you a bit of convenience. Only after a number of years did Bob Noyce start traveling first class—mostly because he was regularly rushing back and forth to Washington, DC, to give congressional testimony on Japanese predations on the chip industry, and he needed to rest up beforehand. We all know it's impossible to sleep in coach.

Intel also stood out in its office design: no "executive row" segregating leadership from the rest of the company; no "executive suites," either. Bob, Andy, Gordon, and the other senior executives' "offices" were standard employee cubicles, double-sized to include their admins' desks, and spread out in different buildings. That a great company would do this validated how we operated at Casto Travel—working side by side, as a team.

Twenty years after they became my client, Intel still structured their office space that way. When Andy offered to say a few words about Casto Travel for our twentieth-anniversary celebration video, our videographer headed over to the Intel campus, excited to meet the Great Andy Grove. Well, he arrived at Intel's main building, in search of Grove's luxurious suite, and instead was directed to the center of a vast, open floor, to Andy's humble cubicle. So much for that. As for Andy, he was Andy: efficient, succinct. He told the videographer, "Sit and I'll tell you exactly what I'm going to say." The shoot took five minutes, and he nailed it on the first take. The videographer wanted to do it again, hoping perhaps to chat a bit. Instead, Andy announced, "That's it. Go."

That was Andy Grove in a nutshell. He told you what he wanted you to do—and you did it. If you did well, he rarely complimented you. But if you screwed up, my God, did you hear about it. This is why, when people found out I worked closely with Andy, they'd say, "I don't know why you aren't scared of him. Everybody else is." Honestly, I didn't see anything to be scared of.

To understand Andy—and I was in the business of understanding my clients—you had to understand where he came from. Born into a Jewish family in Budapest, Hungary, at age four, Andy came down with a near-fatal case of scarlet fever that left him half deaf. A few years later, in 1944, his childhood was shattered when Nazis overthrew the Hungarian government and began rounding up Jews, sending them to death camps or subjecting them to slave labor. Andy's father was forced to serve in the German Army, while Andy and his mother went into hiding under false names, with a Christian family. During his formative years, Andy witnessed unspeakable horrors, in an environment where the slightest slipup meant death. The man who would title his business book *Only the Paranoid Survive* made it out of Hungary by paying attention to even the slightest of details, making every right move and none of the wrong ones. He exceeded even the highest of expectations and perpetually drove himself forward to the next opportunity. Is it any wonder where Andy Grove's demanding nature came from?

Though we had wildly different demeanors at work, Andy and I were alike in our exacting standards, intolerance of mistakes, hatred of failure, and constant search for improvement. Maybe that's why we became such good friends.

THE IMMIGRANTS

Through Intel, not only did Casto Travel gain its first client, but MarDell and I met some of our favorite people, including another Hungarian, Les Vadasz. Intel's third employee and executive vice president, Les had, like Andy, grown up in Budapest during World War II. With his family, he was relocated to a Jewish ghetto for the duration of the war, then released into a tumultuous postwar Hungary, eventually immigrating to the United States via Canada.

Though my background had none of the trauma theirs did, Les, Andy, and I all had immigrated when we were around the same age, and we bonded over that. We all spoke with accents, we all understood what it meant to leave the home of your birth and walk into the unknown, we all had landed in this magical valley, which felt like it was meant to be our home all along, and we were all dedicated to lifting our companies to great heights. Like so many immigrants, we cherished our families here and abroad—in fact, Andy called his mother every single day—and we welcomed the chance to help each other out. These commonalities formed the basis of our friendships, which deepened as our families intertwined.

Judy Vadasz, Les's wife, joined the Casto Travel team as the sales manager in our San Francisco office. She was terrific at the job. Then her father signed on—as had members of my own family—to provide customer care at the airport. With his Old World manners and his experience with Silicon Valley "royalty," he was one of the reasons no one could touch Casto Travel when it came to client services.

As for Andy, he and Eva—his wife and hidden strength, whom I came to adore—entrusted me with planning their family vacations, and in the process, our families integrated, often meeting up on the ski slopes in Lake Tahoe, where we both had houses.

Seeing Andy in both his worlds affirmed what I tried to practice in my own: when you're on the job, give it everything you have, but when you are at home, drop work and focus on family and friends.

Lesson: Never lose sight of your family and friends.

Regardless of his workload, every month, Andy set aside time to have a private dinner with each of his daughters. He took a keen interest in Marc's development, too, asking after his school and career plans, mentoring him, treating him like the son he never had—a connection that remained for the rest of Andy's life.

Yes, this scariest of bosses also had a heart of gold.

LOYALTY

If Andy's heart was gold, his loyalty was steel.

At one point, Casto Travel lost a large portion of the Intel account to a bigger agency, based in South Dakota, owned by Hal Rosenbluth, whom I knew from the industry. Soon after, Robert Wise, director of *The Sound of Music*, was coming to San Jose for an event celebrating the film. I arranged to host a dinner party for him and Millicent, his wife, at my house. I invited two vice presidents of United Airlines to attend, and in the spirit of friendly competition, I called Hal Rosenbluth and said, "Hal, Andy and Eva Grove are coming to dinner at my place. If you want, come on out and join us." He was so excited that he immediately booked a flight from Rapid City.

We had the dinner party outside, and I purposely sat Andy beside Hal so they could meet in person. Well, just as they were starting the pleasantries, the men from United Airlines showed up, saw Andy chatting with Hal, and pulled me aside, demanding, "What's going on?"

I explained, "Hal now has the Intel corporate account, but I'm still working with the VIPs."

They were stunned. One asked, "Why would you invite your replacement to such an important dinner party?"

Before I could answer, I heard Andy ask, "So, what do you do, Hal?"

Hal replied, "Well, I'm the president and owner of Rosenbluth, your new travel agency."

Andy looked at Hal as if he'd said he was from Mars, then he said firmly, "You're not my agent." He pointed at me. "*This* is my agent, and that's not going to change."

That's the kind of loyalty Andrew Grove had for his friends.

He'd signed on as Casto's first client because he knew I would take good care of him. But somewhere along the way, his concern shifted from securing a perfectly executed travel plan to the success of Casto Travel. He became one of my strongest advocates and closest advisers.

Back to the question I never answered that night: Why did I invite Hal Rosenbluth to my dinner party? Because he earned it. His firm had won the Intel contract fair and square. The simple facts were that Intel was now a global firm, Casto Travel wasn't big enough to serve the company properly, and Rosenbluth Travel was.

Besides, we had kept the Intel VIPs, and that's where the big profits were—not just in business trips but in personal travel. Rosenbluth was left with a huge number of potential employee clients, but given they all would be traveling coach, Hal would have to make his profits in volume. So, why fight? Both of us could do a better job—and learn from each other—by working together. Meanwhile, Intel received from the two of us the best possible service.

Lesson: You can never provide customers with the best possible service by yourself—you can only do so by working with others, including your competitors.

I had another reason for welcoming Rosenbluth to Intel: Casto had become too dependent on their business. Intel dominated our revenues, and while that had contributed in an important way to our growth, it also scared me.

I had seen too many travel agencies come to depend upon a single large client, then, when they could no longer serve that client effectively—or the client itself got into financial trouble—they lost the client, revenues dried up, and the agency shuttered.

Lesson: Some companies die from indigestion, not starvation.

I worried that our dependence upon Intel, as great as its success had been, might eventually ruin us. So, while I still entered into the biannual competition for its mainstream travel business, I was secretly relieved when we lost it to Rosenbluth. Now we were free to fight for other big clients. In future years, I would do the same with clients that threatened to distort our business, notably Apple, which I shared with American Express.

WELCOME ADVICE

Interacting with Intel leaders, I learned a lot through observation and osmosis. Who needs business school when you have regular access to insider conversations between some of the greatest business minds around? I also learned how to—and how not to—engage advisers, beginning with Andy.

As Casto Travel expanded and I began hiring people into executive roles, I found myself uncharacteristically indecisive. I would receive resumes laden with business school credentials, internships, and impressive work histories—none of which I had—and somehow that short-circuited my ability to discern the right candidate for the job. So, I'd call up Andy and say, "I'm interviewing someone, and I could really use your insight." I'd give him the details, and he'd say, "Okay, I'll interview them."

Imagine, for a moment, applying for a job in an up-and-coming travel agency, and the person conducting your vetting interview is Andy Grove.

Anyway, on one occasion, I asked Andy to vet a candidate for vice president. Andy came back and said, "Don't hire this guy. He is the wrong person for you." Well, me being me, I didn't take his advice—and it turned out to be a disaster.

Lesson: Nobody is above looking to others for acquired wisdom.

In fact, during that period, I didn't follow Andy's hiring advice on *four* different occasions. Finally, he got fed up with me and said, "Look, don't call me. Don't ask me, because you never take my advice."

I barked back, "Well, what do you know about the hospitality business? What do you know about customer service?"

He was forever telling me, "You have to look for *this* expertise in a person, *this* competency, not the credentials." Needless to say, he was usually right.

Lesson: Don't be dazzled by credentials; what matters is proven competence.

But when he wasn't right, I didn't hesitate to tell him that. On my turf, I didn't brook any nonsense, not even from Andy Grove. He'd say, "You're not doing it right. Let me tell you what you should do."

I'd counter, "You don't know what you're talking about. Let me do it this way and then you'll see."

Then he'd call me and say, "You know, you were right."

I'd reply, "Of course I'm right. When it comes to the travel busi-ness, you really don't know what you're talking about. I don't tell you how to do your business, don't tell me how to do mine."

In retrospect, I was likely one among very few people who told Andy Grove he didn't know what he was talking about, but we had that kind of relationship. We were equally bullheaded, and we respected each other. We told each other the truth, and as much as we might have argued about this approach or that, he remained a trusted adviser to the end.

Eventually, I learned that "looking for core competencies" applied to vetting advisers as well as potential employees. When I built my advisory board, I asked Irwin Federman, CEO of Monolithic Memories, Inc., to join because of his financial expertise—he could identify a potential problem at a glance and just as quickly see a way to address it. Bob Noyce brought to the board his expansive vision and optimism. Mario Rosati, of Wilson Sonsini Goodrich & Rosati, contributed his invaluable legal perspective. Bill Bowes, legendary venture capitalist and founder of U.S. Venture Partners, brought his stellar reputation, his vast knowledge of established and upcoming Valley companies, and his even-keeled personality. Bill was always the mature guy in the room—he listened to everyone, he treated everyone with respect, and as a result, he had a calming influence. Each member of the board brought something unique to the table, and as a whole, this A-list of Silicon Valley players gave Casto Travel enormous credibility in the eyes of the world. They were all so generous with their time, and I cer-tainly listened to what they had to say, but I still made my own deci-sions. They understood and respected that about me.

What I always found invaluable was connecting with business leaders who were in the same boat I was. Though they specialized in tech and I in travel, we rode the ups and downs of the same economy, and our businesses expanded and contracted in tandem with each other. Just knowing they had gone through some of the same growing pains I was experiencing—and had survived—gave me great comfort. I remember confiding in Intel founder Bob Noyce once, "Bob, I'm get-ting really nervous because my company is just growing so fast, and I don't have a business plan."

"Oh, Maryles," Bob said, "it took us a while to have a business plan for Intel, too."

Keep in mind, he was talking about the fastest-growing company in the world at that moment. I don't know if he said it just because he wanted to reassure me, but he made me feel like, *Oh my God, these guys didn't know what they were doing, either.*

Then Bob added, "Don't worry about it. You'll be okay." That kind of reassurance meant the world to me.

Whatever situation I found myself in, I knew if I phoned these pillars of Intel—Les, Andy, or Bob—my calls would always get through. Often I solicited their advice not because I didn't know what to do but because I wanted to vet my plans or hear how they would handle situations. People are so willing to teach if you ask them, and I did, storing their ideas in my box of memories, to pull out if and when I needed them.

Of course, as any businesswoman will tell you, sometimes people will want to teach even when you *don't* ask them—a trait we call "mansplaining" today. In those cases, I didn't take unsolicited advice as an insult to my intelligence, nor did I feel I had to speak up to prove myself. Instead, I put my airline training to work and used listening as a powerful business tool. Hospitality is all about understanding people so you can help them feel welcome, comfortable, seen, and heard. That begins not with talking but with listening—the superpower that ensured Casto Travel's success.

Lesson: You can't listen when you're talking.

SURVIVOR

Without Intel, there would have been no Casto Travel. That didn't mean that my firm and Intel had a smooth relationship. As Intel grew at a dizzying pace, we moved from interacting with executive secretaries to working with the purchasing department, and our lives at Casto Travel became miserable. That department treated us exactly as it did every contractor: brutally. Unreasonable requests. Impossible deadlines. Somehow, though we had gained the iron-clad loyalty of the impossible-to-please CEO, Andy, we never earned the esteem of the people in purchasing. I not only had to compete regularly with every other agency vying for their business, I had to do one notch better. Sometimes I felt like, *You know what? It's not worth it. To hell with these people.* But I needed them, and they needed me. In the end, what redeemed our work over twenty-five years were my relationships with Andy, Bob, Gordon, and Les, among other executives. I couldn't let them down.

Lesson: Loyalty is a two-way street.

Though the purchasing department gave me more than my fair share of headaches, my friendships with Intel's leaders gave me some of the most memorable experiences of my life. More on those in a bit.

My mother, Caridad, a beautiful woman to match her beautiful heart.

My family, Christmas 1958. Standing (left to right): Maryles, Marilen, Antonia, my mother, father, and Tony. Kneeling: Agustin, Jose Mari, Rafael Jr.

My rebellious years in school.

Queen of the day.
Got the crown but
not the boy.

I get my wings, and
the flying days begin.

First date, 1964: me and MarDell—the stars are aligned.

Lee Michaels—my partner.

First office: ferns, maps, repo depo desk . . . let the business begin!

Open house with first team and eagerly awaiting Marc's arrival.

Marc and our "first" Casto meeting.

The 3 M's: MarDell, Maryles, and Marc.

Daddy in his office.

MarDell and Marc on board the Castoways to Hawaii.

Above: MarDell and Bob tinkering with Bob's new underwater camera creation. Left: Eva and Andy celebrating Casto's twenty-first wedding anniversary.

Bill Perry—an exceptional man making this world a better place.

1980 work, play, and baby, too, at Casto office. Janice, Terre, and Erin.

Beth, kicked out of Apple for her original version of the ticket delivery outfit, "Oh Well."

Casto office, umbrellas and all.

The partners, Marc, me, and Gus.

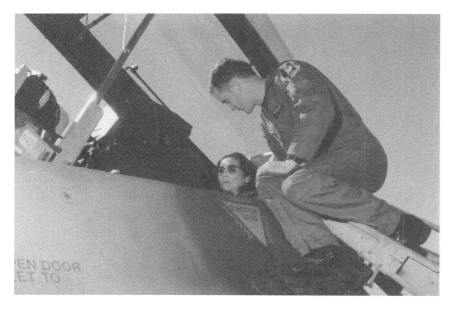

Looking for a hole in the clouds on an F-16 Fighting Falcon in the "Nine-G" environment.

Marc, you light up my life.

Flying off to new adventures.

Casto girls, Grandma's bookends.

CHAPTER 6

THE INTIMIDATION FACTOR

As anyone who went to Catholic school in the 1950s will tell you, if you're not intimidated by nuns, you're unlikely to be cowed by anyone. Well, the Silicon Valley I came up in was full of characters whose brutality rivaled that of the meanest ruler-wielding nuns. But remember the boarding school garbage-can incident? I was ready for them.

I once asked Andy Grove, "How come people are so frightened of you?" He couldn't give me an answer. Later, I flipped that question around: Why wasn't I intimidated by him? I can think of a few reasons.

If there was one overarching truth about Andy Grove, it was that he never lied. He never sugarcoated anything. While that could be painful for others—and for him—it also made him trustworthy. I always knew exactly what he thought and how he felt.

Add to that the fact that Andy—along with the rest of the Valley's known intimidators—was my client, not my boss. So, if I screwed up, I might lose an important client—and that would have been problematic for Casto Travel—but I would not lose my livelihood. I trusted in my ability to survive with or without Intel or any of my other key clients. Perhaps I would have felt differently if the stakes were higher, if Andy had been my boss, but the bottom line remains the same: no one can take away the qualities that make me who I am, and I can trust in those qualities to help me build back up if ever I get torn down.

Lesson: Remember who you are.

Additionally, by example, my father taught me that "intimidating" is a role people play. Over and over again, I watched him adopt his hyperstrict personality—as the head of a business and as the head of a household full of wild children—only to drop it in more relaxed circumstances. I saw the same in my notoriously brusque clients and friends.

Lesson: If you look at the whole person, you'll see most everyone has a softer side.

Deep down, everyone wants to be understood. So, in my interactions with all people, I try to see beyond their masks to the essence of their humanity, and I form my relationships there.

When you connect with someone's humanness, you realize that no matter how successful, wealthy, influential, or famous people are, they're still just people. That's why I never thought of myself as any different from them. In fact, we were a lot alike—ambitious, success driven, always pushing for the next horizon, experts in our domains. In that sense, we all belonged to the same club. I worked just as hard as they did, and like them, I had power and I knew how to use it. So what if some of them had big voices? I had a big voice, too.

Lesson: Sometimes if you weather the bark, you'll learn there is no bite.

Take Irwin Federman, who served on the Casto advisory board, for example. He had joined MMI as the CFO and stepped into the company's top seat when founder Ze'ev Drori, an Israeli scientist, was fired. The semiconductor industry was such a complicated business—more physics than electronics—that its leaders had always been scientist-entrepreneurs. With an accountant now at the helm, most tech pundits predicted Federman, and MMI, would fail. On the contrary, Irwin, who became a Casto client, did brilliantly not only at MMI but later as a venture capitalist and chairman of SanDisk.

Personality-wise, Irwin Federman was a brusque, brutally honest man who didn't suffer fools lightly. When I turned to him for financial advice, he always wanted just the facts, and he wanted them quickly. If I took the long way around, he'd say, "Get to the point, Maryles. Get to the damn point." But he'd always listen and share his perspective. Like Andy, Irwin invested himself in Casto Travel's success and celebrated our milestones, even making a beautiful speech at our fortieth-anniversary party. Like so many others, underneath that gruff exterior, Irwin is a very kind person and remains a trusted friend.

Though I encountered many challenging personalities over the years, none compared to Silicon Valley's most notorious: Steve Jobs.

L'ENFANT TERRIBLE

Casto Travel's connection to Apple Computer came along several pathways, all converging in 1980. First, an executive admin from National Semiconductor, who had worked with Casto, moved over to Apple and contacted us about taking her boss on as a personal client. Then Ann Bowers—a dear friend who married Intel founder Bob Noyce in a different kind of Silicon Valley merger—joined Apple as the company's first vice president of human resources. Finally, I had worked with, and knew well, Apple's chairman, A.C. "Mike" Markkula Jr., who had retired after a successful career at Intel and joined up with these two kids, Steve Wozniak and Steve Jobs.

When Casto signed on, Apple was in the process of becoming a publicly traded company, riding the success of the Apple II, the world's first preassembled, mass-produced personal computer. By the end of 1980, they had sold a hundred thousand Apple IIs, but more importantly, they had whet the market's appetite for personal computers. It took a few months, but eventually, I landed the department I wanted there: sales and marketing. Not long after that, I had my first encounter with Steve Jobs.

Today, Jobs stands as one of the titanic figures of our time—the public face of a team that launched a technological revolution, a visionary inventor and strategic mastermind, a role model to generations of designers, engineers, and entrepreneurs. Jobs's most enduring image—emaciated body, round glasses, thinning hair, like an ascetic monk—is recognized around the world. Not as recognizable is the Jobs of the 1980s—the stunning young man with the hawkish face, thick black hair, and knowing smile. That's who I met—a man celebrated and feared, arrogant and troubled.

Behind the mythical reputation Jobs earned at the end of his life—which has only grown since—runs an undercurrent of complaint: he was a megalomaniac, he was cruel, he took credit for others' hard work. In my experience, he was not one or the other, he was both—the most paradoxical, remarkable, and infuriating person I've ever known.

My first contact with Steve Jobs came via a telephone call from San Jose Airport. The second I put the receiver to my ear, I heard screaming on the other end—including some choice vocabulary I had learned from my downstairs neighbor in Upland but hadn't heard since. Why was he angry to the point of screaming profanities at a woman he didn't know? Because he had arrived at the airport to find that he was flying to the East Coast on a smaller airplane than he'd expected. That was it. After unleashing his string of profanities, he demanded, "Why did you book me on this plane?"

"That's the plane the airline uses for the flight you requested," I replied.

That wasn't the answer he wanted, so he continued ranting.

I didn't need to waste my time listening to this, so I cut to the chase. "Do you want me to book you on a different flight?" I asked.

More raging: No, he didn't want a different *flight*; he wanted *this* flight but with a different *plane*.

My God, I thought. *I'm dealing with a tantruming child.* I held the phone away from my ear, imagining what a sight he must have been to the people walking by in the terminal. Finally, I said, "I'll tell you what, Steve, do you want me to book a private plane for you?"

That quieted him. "No," he said. "I just—"

I cut him off. "So why are you screaming?" That's when I hung up on him. No one was going to abuse me like that.

Lesson: Draw your line and hold it. You don't have to take the abuse.

Now, I'm not sure, but history may record that I was the only person to hang up on Steve Jobs. Regardless, a few minutes later, he called back. By this time, he had calmed down. "Well," he said, "just get me on a different plane."

"Look," I replied, "don't argue with me. There's nothing we can do now. The airline is not going to change the plane for you because you don't like the size of it. So, do you want to take this flight, or do you want to book a different one? That's it, make a decision."

Lesson: Don't get distracted by the bullying behavior; instead, iden-tify the problem and seek a solution.

In the end, he took the flight, but not before he'd told me—in the rudest terms possible—exactly how he felt about it.

From that day on, I was wary of Steve Jobs, for good reason. In the years that followed, though my conversations with him were relatively polite—at least compared to that first one—I sensed a tinge of menace in his words, as if he might go off again at any minute. Always I kept in mind the underlying truth about these Masters of the Universe personality types: how frightened many of them are inside, how many had been catered to despite their impossible behaviors, and how much of their success had come from luck rather than skill.

For all of its glory, even Apple needed luck at the beginning. I once told Steve, "My God, if I had gotten the same funding you did, where would I be? What would you have done if you weren't funded—if others didn't give you a pile of money, and instead you had to start from zero? You got where you are at least partly because someone wrote you a check. You couldn't have done what I did." Steve didn't like that, but he didn't disagree.

Over time, I saw Steve's softer side, too. Once, he brought his family to a skating party Eva Grove and her sister hosted each year. I watched Steve take to the rink with his youngest daughter, who was just learning to skate. He was so tender with her, holding her hand, encouraging her as she inched forward. Seeing that vulnerable side—one he almost never showed in public—made me think differently of him.

For all of the wariness between us, Steve could, when he was alone, drop his predator persona. As part of Casto's service, we not only arranged Steve's flights and ground transportation, but when I could, I went along to make sure things went smoothly at the airport. On one of those trips, in the back of a limousine headed to SFO, Steve and I started talking about business, and me being me, I mentioned a decision I was considering, just to see what he'd say.

"I'm thinking of taking Casto Travel public," I told him.

Unexpectedly, Steve looked me in the eye and became very sincere. "Maryles," he said, "if you don't have to, *don't*. It changes everything that happens in the company."

I'd like to think Steve and I developed a respect for—if not a trust in—each other over the years. Not long after he had been fired from Apple, he called me up and asked to see me. When we met, the hurt over his breakup with the company he had founded was clear—I could sense it as much as I could see it in his face. He told me, "Maryles, I'm starting this new company called NeXT. I want you to be our agent." Even after suffering a humiliating fall from grace, ousted by the CEO he'd recruited, he was determined to come back. A lesser personality might have hidden—but not Steve Jobs. I admired his resolve.

Yet, I never forgot that the other Steve was always waiting to reemerge. Once, I accompanied him to the Admirals Club lounge at SFO. When we arrived, he suddenly decided he needed to unpack and repack his entire suitcase and garment bag. So, he flung them open and began his project right in the middle of the lounge area, taking up way more than his fair share of space. Annoyed, other guests came up to me to complain. So, I went to Steve and demanded, "What are you doing?"

"I'm packing," he said without looking up.

"You can't do that out here," I insisted. "You need to take it to that room over there." I pointed to a nearby doorway.

Unmoved, he said, "Well, I want to do it here."

I could tell Steve was about to have another of his tantrums, and I had learned how to deal with them by then: directly. I was adamant, and Steve finally moved to the other room. The angry looks from everyone else probably helped motivate him—even Steve Jobs wasn't immune to embarrassment.

Sometimes Steve's vulnerability and arrogance would operate at the same time—which would have been charming if it weren't also infuriating. Once—before his marriage to Laurene Powell—on a Lufthansa flight between Frankfurt and London, Steve struck up a conversation with a woman sitting beside him. He was smitten, but for some reason, he hadn't thought to ask for her name, much less her phone number, so he called me. "Maryles," he begged, "you've got to find her, you've got to find her." He sounded desperate, like this woman was the one.

"Okay, okay," I told him. Who was I to stand in the way of love? So, we scrambled to find her.

In those days, passenger lists were not automated, so "finding her" meant contacting Lufthansa and calling in every favor I had to get them to go through the passenger manifest and find out the name of the woman who had been seated beside Steve.

It took three days.

Finally, I got the name. I was so excited. I called Steve. "Hey, guess what? We found her name!"

Steve was puzzled. "Whose name?"

"What do you mean 'Whose name'?" I asked, my voice rising. "The woman you were seated next to on your flight, the one you *had* to find."

"Oh, I forgot about it."

Now it was my turn to swear. "Goddamn it. You put me through hell. I used all of my contacts to try to get that name, and you don't even remember?"

"No," was all he said.

But that was Steve—sending us on a three-day goose chase to serve a momentary impulse; and that was Casto Travel—doing everything we could to keep our clients happy.

RESILIENCE

In the early days of Apple, I was impressed by how many women held positions of power: Debi Coleman, who joined as the financial controller for the Macintosh division in 1981; Sue Cook, who onboarded in 1982 and founded Apple University with Ann Bowers; and Ellen Hancock, who served as chief technology officer beginning in 1995. In the boys' club of Silicon Valley, these women stood out like a beacon of hope.

But over time, I learned their success had come at considerable cost. Steve Jobs treated them horribly, screamed at them, humiliated them, called them idiots and much worse. These remarkable women. It was unconscionable. Some might say, "Steve did that to everybody," but I believe he reserved a special level of abuse for the women. How do I know? Because they confided in me, often through tears. I wonder, even in those days, if the Valley had known the extent of the abuse, would Jobs have gotten away with it?

After three years of this, in 1984, Debi Coleman transferred out of Steve's department to manage the manufacturing plant in Fremont. In 1986, after Steve was fired, she became Apple Computer's chief financial officer.

As for Sue Cook, she stayed on for nearly three years, leaving in 1985 to bring her visionary leadership skills to the Tom Peters Company. Then she branched out on her own, founding Think consulting. One can only imagine what more she could have done for Apple had the work environment changed.

But no one was treated worse—or deserved it less—than Ellen Hancock. Former senior vice president of IBM, executive vice president and COO of National Semiconductor, Ellen had as impressive a career as any woman in the history of tech. But not long after her arrival at Apple in 1996, she made a decision that had far-reaching consequences.

When Steve Jobs heard Apple was hunting for a next-generation operating system for the Mac, he appeared on the Apple campus for the first time since his ouster to push for his new company's product, NeXTSTEP. As the CTO, Ellen favored a different operating system, but under great pressure from Jobs, Apple settled on NeXTSTEP, against her recommendation.

Well, buying NeXT brought Jobs back to Apple, and from that day on, he embarked on a campaign to destroy Ellen Hancock. He publicly ridiculed her, calling her a "bozo" and a "moron." He pushed the CEO to strip Ellen of her primary duties, replacing her with his allies. To the outside world, Ellen, a twenty-eight-year tech veteran, handled these attacks with enormous strength and grace, but as her friend, I saw the other side. I remember her sobbing in my living room over the injustices wielded by Steve Jobs.

Behavior like this—it's not just "intimidating," it's cruel, it's inexcusable, it leaves deep scars, it undercuts the effectiveness of invaluable employees, and these days, it puts a company in danger of litigation. Many companies have made great strides in eradicating such abuses, or firing the people who perpetrate them, which I applaud. But I want to point something else out, too.

I think it's important to note the resilience of these women—of all the people who have met angry wolves on their paths and somehow continued on. Yes, Steve Jobs may have rerouted, disrupted, or derailed Debi, Sue, and Ellen's—and who knows how many other women's—tenures at Apple, but each of these powerful women ultimately prevailed, finding success on her own terms.

Lesson: Whether you choose to stay the course or try a different path, anywhere you go, your strengths, abilities, and talents go with you.

Yes, bullying behaviors can make a workplace intolerable, and I hope you never encounter them. But if you do, rest assured that the same reputation, expertise, and skills that got you hired in the first place will either help you move through the challenge, land you a job somewhere else, or serve you well when you take the entrepreneurial leap and head out on your own.

CHAPTER 7

THE YIN AND YANG
OF THE VALLEY

What is a legacy? Some think it is the work you have done. Others believe it is the way you treat people. I say the two are not mutually exclusive: it's both. To me, what matters is not a person's success but the way a person carries that success—a value I learned from my parents. Certainly, from my vantage point in Silicon Valley, I watched people carry their successes in vastly different ways. Nowhere did I see this more clearly than on a trip I took to Los Angeles.

AWARD NIGHT

As one of United Airlines' top vendors, one year, I was invited by the company to attend the Academy Awards—a great honor and an affirmation of the esteem Casto Travel had gained in the travel industry. Hosted by a vice president of the airline, our party included John Chambers, CEO of Cisco Systems, and his wife, philanthropist Elaine Chambers. Also present was Oracle chairman Larry Ellison, who, in keeping with his reputation, brought as his date a spectacularly gorgeous woman who looked like she might pop out of her gown at any moment.

The evening began with a cocktail party at our hotel, after which the six of us headed out to the lobby to wait for our limousine. When it arrived, as we walked toward the curb, the driver got out and opened the passenger door. Larry and his date climbed in first, then as the rest of us moved to follow, Larry looked out at us and said, "No, I don't ride with anyone else." He slammed the door shut and ordered the driver to leave us.

The four of us were left standing there, jaws dropped. I couldn't believe the arrogance of the man. I had heard stories, but now I saw it in person. Keep in mind that on Academy Awards night, just about every limousine in the Los Angeles Basin is taken, so Larry didn't just strand us there, he put our limousine service on the spot as well. Luckily, after much scrambling, they finally found a replacement.

As that car arrived and we climbed in, a button popped on John Chambers's jacket. Now, here is the difference between someone like Larry Ellison and an old-fashioned Southern gentleman like John Chambers. John asked if the driver might wait a minute, then he jumped out of the limo, ran upstairs to his room, and grabbed its emergency sewing kit. When he returned to the car, he apologized for the delay, and as we drove off, he set about sewing the loose button back on himself.

I remember thinking, *My God, there is the yin and yang of Silicon Valley.*

While certain qualities are essential to an entrepreneur's success—vision, ambition, risk tolerance—arrogance is not one of them.

Lesson: You don't have to be a jerk to be successful.

Fortunately, I worked with considerably more Chamberses than Ellisons, a few of whom I'd like to remember here.

THE LAWMAKER

For a man who was present at every major event in the founding of the digital age, whose namesake law is the measure and metronome of the modern world, Gordon Moore remained the most humble, gracious, and down-to-earth of Silicon Valley's forefathers. In fact, I didn't have many business dealings with Gordon because his idea of a vacation, even when he ranked among the wealthiest people in California, was to jump in his camper van with Betty, his wife, and head up into the mountains to a favorite fishing spot.

Instead, the Moores and I got to know each other socially, especially when they bought a house near mine in Hawaii, where Betty stayed for health reasons while Gordon traveled back and forth to California until his career wound down to retirement. Whenever I was at the Hawaii house, I'd make a point of visiting Betty, and Gordon, if he was in town.

To me, the experience that most captured Gordon's personality was a dinner that MarDell and I shared with the Moores at a local restaurant. When it came time to order wine, Gordon chose the cheapest on the menu—Meridian—not because of the price but because he liked it. The waiter, who knew Gordon by reputation, barely contained his surprise over the request. Who knows if the restaurant even had a bottle on hand? Likely no one had ordered it in years. I imagined the waiter running out the back door to a nearby grocery store to grab one.

That was the kind of person Gordon was—so unpretentious you would never guess his wealth. Betty once said to me, "I can't believe all the people I've met all over the world because I was Gordon's wife." She was in awe of what happened in their lives, but neither she nor Gordon was changed by it. I loved that about them.

COMMON TOUCH

Similarly, William J. Perry never lost his common touch. President and founder of Electromagnetic Systems Laboratory (ESL), where he became a Casto client, his work in the areas of signals intelligence, surveillance capabilities, and stealth aircraft technology won him the respect of the Department of Defense, where he served as a technical consultant, then as undersecretary for research. In the early eighties, he returned to San Francisco as managing director of investment banking firm Hambrecht & Quist, where he stayed until 1985, when he returned to Washington, DC, playing a series of different roles before ultimately serving as Secretary of Defense under President Clinton. Those are just a few highlights from his storied career, but here's what really impressed me about Bill Perry: he remained the same salt-of-the-earth person, no matter his role.

When he was running ESL, if he wanted to book a personal trip, he wouldn't tell someone else to call me—he'd just jump into his pickup truck and drive over to meet me. We'd sit down together and plan out the whole trip. When he was Secretary of Defense, he would still personally call me to make his reservations.

I have to admit, it was impressive to have my phone intercom announce, "The Pentagon is calling." The whole office would be abuzz—*the Pentagon!* I'd pick up the receiver and hear, "Dr. Perry is calling." Then Bill would come on, and it was just like it had always been.

No matter his accomplishments, as an inventor, a business leader, a civil servant, a fellow at the Hoover Institution, or a professor at Stanford, Bill Perry remained the same decent individual he'd always been. That's why, as with John Chambers and Intel founder Bob Noyce, Bill holds a special place in my heart. They were three of the most brilliant, humble, and gracious people to represent Silicon Valley.

Lesson: No matter your success, never lose your humility.

THE MAYOR OF SILICON VALLEY

Robert Noyce's name may not be instantly recognizable to people outside the tech world, but his influence on the Valley and world was—and still is—immeasurable. A founder of Fairchild Semiconductor, then Intel, he invented the first integrated monolithic circuit chip made of silicon, hence the Valley's name. But it was Bob's personality that earned him the nickname the Mayor of Silicon Valley. Now, I may not be intimidated by fame, but I was hardly unaffected by Bob's legendary charisma. With his athletic presence, his deep voice, and his incredible intellect, he owned every room he entered, even a church. The child of a Nebraska preacher, Bob had sung in the choir, and as a dear family friend, he would sing at our Christmas gatherings, with his beautiful baritone voice.

Like Bill Perry, Bob was one of the most centered human beings I've ever met. Lobbying in the halls of Congress, addressing an industry convention, or on vacation on a Pacific island, he never changed. He had no personas that he hauled out as needed; he was what he was—and that was a very nice person. At work, he was known for encouraging a relaxed atmosphere, treating employees as family, and inspiring and rewarding teamwork.

Bob once said, "Optimism is an essential ingredient of innovation. How else can the individual welcome change over security, adventure over staying in safe places?" His enthusiasm was infectious—Bob was always up for an adventure, always encouraging me to come along. Is it any wonder that he and MarDell became instant friends? They were like two boys together, bonding over their love of skiing, scuba diving, and flying.

Keeping up with MarDell had always been a challenge, but keeping up with MarDell and Bob? That brought things to a whole new level, which is how I ended up helicopter skiing in the mountains near Reno, Nevada, for the first and only time—yet another adventure I thought might kill me, but I somehow enjoyed, once it was over. After that, I left the helicopter skiing to the boys, which freed them to take on much more dangerous terrain, like the Canadian Bugaboos.

As for scuba diving, I was as enthusiastic about that activity as I had been about skiing at the start. But, undaunted by my resistance, Bob came to my house for scuba lessons in my pool. Then he flew us to Catalina Island—he loved to fly, too—to get our certification. After that, there was no stopping us.

Exotic vacations with the Noyces became a regular part of our lives. My contribution was to plan the best experience I could. We traveled to the Philippines, New Guinea, Bali, the Great Barrier Reef, the Caribbean—always taking a new diving adventure. Not surprisingly, the inventor of the integrated circuit was also an inveterate tinkerer. I still have a photograph of Bob and MarDell with this enormous underwater camera Bob had built and lugged around on our Caribbean island dives.

Our vacation fun wasn't restricted to the ocean, though. Even shopping became memorable with Bob. At a market in New Guinea, Bob was intrigued by a carved banana-shaped wooden bowl. He waved it around, showing it to everybody, until he was informed it was a well-used, antique codpiece. He dropped it as if it were electrified.

Once in Bali with the Noyces and the Vesdaszs, we visited another open market where I saw Bob about to buy an item for full price. I said to him, "Don't do that. You've got to haggle; they expect you to."

Bob said, "These people don't have any money. I should pay them the full amount." In his business life, Bob, famously, had a hard time firing even the worst employee. I'd believed that was because he was uncomfortable with conflict, but after seeing him refuse to negotiate in the market that day, I realized it was as much about empathy and generosity.

Still, I pushed him, saying, "Bob, don't go American on me, okay? We're having fun here." So, I took over the haggling while he watched. I got him a good deal. For all I know, though, Bob may have slipped the vendor some extra cash.

Bob was as spontaneous as he was kind, which led to all kinds of unforeseen turns of events and unexpected generosities. Once, after a lunch celebrating the distribution of Casto's annual profit sharing, Bob and I were driving down Stevens Creek Boulevard in San Jose, the region's "auto row," when I spotted a used car. "Bob!" I shouted. "Stop! There's a Mercedes-Benz in that lot. I want to see it!" Bob immediately pulled in.

The car was a black Mercedes-Benz 280SL "pagoda top" convertible. Thanks to the profit distribution, I had some extra cash, but when the salesman told me the price—ten thousand dollars—that seemed a bit high. Forgetting Bob's track record with haggling, I nudged him and whispered, "Negotiate the price."

In the end, I suppose he did, but not in the way I expected him to. Instead of talking the salesman down on my black car, Bob pointed to a beige 280SL next to it and asked in his booming voice, "How about that one? Is it for sale?"

The salesman said, "Yes."

"Fine," said Bob. "I'll buy it."

As a result, we got both cars, with a three-thousand-dollar discount. When I pulled out my little checkbook—it would take most of what I had in the bank—Bob told me to pay only seven thousand dollars. He paid full price, while I got my deal. That was Bob. How could anyone not love a person like that?

For years afterward, Bob would call me out of the blue and say, in that unmistakable voice, "Hey, let's drive our cars." I'd drop everything and we'd race along the winding roads of Silicon Valley's surrounding hills in our little roadsters. As much as anyone I've ever met, Bob Noyce made life fun.

That's why he and MarDell were such a great match. When their shared love of high-risk activities surpassed Ann's and mine, they took off without us. When Bob bought a seaplane in Boston and needed to get it to California, instead of hiring a crew to ferry it west, he and MarDell decided to take a few days to fly it across the country themselves, landing each night in various bodies of water. Well, on one leg of the trip, Ann and I each got a call from Colorado. As if they had rehearsed a script, both Bob and MarDell casually explained, "We're having a little engine trouble and we need to wait for repairs. We'll be home a few days late." Only after they arrived home did we learn the full truth: that "engine trouble" had forced an emergency landing. Later, I saw a picture of the damage—this wasn't just a few scratches from brushing the treetops. They had crashed the plane. More so, they had sunk the plane in a lake. Ever the charismatic personalities, the two of them convinced a couple of kids in a pickup truck with a winch to help them pull it to dry ground where they could conduct repairs. Of course, Bob and MarDell fixed the engine—which they had suspended from a nearby tree—themselves.

MarDell's friendship with Bob—and their shenanigans—continued after he and Ann moved to Austin, Texas, where Bob took over leadership of SEMATECH, a research-and-development consortium formed by fourteen US semiconductor firms and the US government. Bob didn't really want the job, but he understood the importance of the consortium—he'd led the fight for its formation in Congress—and no one else wanted the job, either. He felt duty bound to step up, so he did. It was a very Bob Noyce thing to do.

In 1990, the Mayor of Silicon Valley, the man who had seemed the healthiest and strongest of tech's early founders, went for a swim in his pool in Austin, suffered a massive heart attack, and died. He was sixty-three years old. News of Bob's death sent a shock wave through

Silicon Valley. The shock was even greater at our house, where Bob had been an integral part of our daily lives—MarDell's up-for-anything pal, my dear friend and coconspirator, an adored and adoring presence throughout Marc's childhood. We were all devastated, but none more than MarDell, who Marc remembers seeing slumped in a chair, weeping at the news. Bob's death would transform our family in ways I could not yet see.

Every major figure in technology attended Bob's memorial in Downtown San Jose, as his plane, in which we had made so many wonderful memories, flew by overhead. His absence left a hole in the Valley that no person since has ever quite filled. His legacy—his accomplishments, his optimism, his humility, his kindness—lives on in today's technology and in the hearts of the people he inspired every day.

CHAPTER 8

FINDING MY TRIBE

Despite their wildly different personalities and behaviors, the Silicon Valley founders I have mentioned so far share many common traits: superhuman intelligence, limitless ambition, otherworldly ingenuity, lightning-fast adaptability, and a near-insatiable appetite for high risk and even higher reward. A sign of the times, they also shared one more trait: they were all men. Though I found my place among them—as a highly sought-after contractor, as an entrepreneur myself, and as a friend to some—more often than I can count, at business meetings and industry events, I was the only woman in the room. No wonder, at social functions, I gravitated toward my clients' wives, who were brilliant, fascinating, accomplished women in their own right. Connecting with them soothed a loneliness I wasn't even aware I carried until we met. Whenever I could, I would find opportunities for us to work together on community initiatives, fundraisers, and nonprofit boards.

That loneliness makes sense, if you think about it. At home, I was one woman among three men—my father, my brother, and MarDell— and one boy quickly growing into a man. At work, though the Casto Team became family, I was a solo entrepreneur—I had no true peers. While the work, family, and travel compartments of my life were overflowing, the sisterhood compartment stood nearly empty. I didn't even think to go looking for more women like me until I received an invitation to their club.

THE COMMITTEE OF 200

In 1982, an elite group of businesswomen met for the first time in a conference room in Los Angeles. The invitation list for this gathering was culled from a National Association of Women Business Owners study that identified, among nearly two thousand women who held executive positions across the country, two hundred who either owned companies that grossed at least $5 million or headed up corporations or divisions with more than $20 million in annual sales.

The primary goal for that first meeting was to raise funds for NAWBO, which they did. But something else happened, too: guided by founding organizer Susan Davis, these innovators, influencers, and role models from the highest ranks of business launched the Committee of 200, an organization committed to uniting women entrepreneurs and supporting the advancement of businesswomen.

Founding C200 members included Katharine Graham of the *Washington Post*, Sherry Lansing of 20th Century Studios, Paula D. Hughes of Thomson McKinnon Securities in New York, Jane Evans of General Mills, Edie Fraser of STEMconnector, and Christie Hefner of Playboy Enterprises, among so many others. They represented industries as diverse as banking, construction, fashion, oil, and publishing, and regions stretching from the high-rises of New York City to Louisville, Kentucky, to Silicon Valley. When Casto Travel crossed that $5 million threshold, I was invited to join.

I attended my first C200 conference in San Francisco, and from the moment I stepped through the doors, I was bowled over. Everywhere I looked, there were so many powerful, accomplished women—all wearing name tags, thank goodness, so I could identify who they were. That's how I knew, when I stepped into the elevator, that I was standing between Christie Hefner and fashion designer Wanda Ferragamo. I remember thinking, *What am I doing here with these incredible women?* I quickly learned that Wanda had just come from Rome and didn't speak much English. Well, I knew how that felt, so I stayed with her for a while and helped with translation.

Throughout the conference, with each speech, mealtime conversation, and momentary interaction, I grew to feel more at home. Listening to other women's stories, it finally sunk in: *They're just like me.* We were all succeeding against the odds in our business lives, we all knew the loneliness of leadership, we all understood what it felt like, in a sea full of sport coats and neckties, to be wearing the only skirt in the room. I'd found my tribe.

My favorite conference session was called "Conversations With . . . ," during which one or two C200 members were invited to tell their personal stories. Here we were safe to say anything, without fear of media exposure or the intrusion of outsiders. We could talk about our losses, our confusions, our challenges and missteps, to a room full of people who understood that power and vulnerability aren't opposites, they're two parts of the same whole. At that first meeting, Wanda talked about her husband's death in 1960 and her struggle to take control of the shoe company he started, Salvatore Ferragamo. Christie talked about her more recent experiences, in 1988, stepping into power at Playboy Enterprises. I was blown away.

At the next C200 conference I attended, it was Silicon Valley icon Carol Bartz who caught my attention. In 1983, Carol had come to the Valley from Digital Equipment back East to work at Sun Microsystems. She had been so successful at Sun that she had been recruited to run architectural software company Autodesk, in Marin County. She had turned it into a powerhouse, celebrated for its enlightened employee philosophy.

I met Carol when she first walked into the conference. She looked around, eyes wide, and said, "Good Lord, look at all these women!" There she was in her earthy blue jeans, watching C200 members pass by in their designer suits. "I don't think this is the group for me," she whispered. She may not have stayed with C200 for long, but the story she told that day has remained with me ever since, not only because Carol was funny, sardonic, and swore like a sailor but because it exemplified her resilience.

Just after Carol had accepted her job at Autodesk, she was diagnosed with breast cancer. She didn't tell anyone. Her chemotherapy treatment began days before she started her new job, leaving her weak and nauseated. What did she do? She put on a brave face and drove to work, as scheduled. As she walked up the front steps of Autodesk to appear before the board of directors for the first time in her new role, she had to lean over the rail to vomit in the bushes. Then, with the toughness that became her hallmark, she straightened herself up and marched into the meeting.

Hearing Carol's story, I marveled over all the impossibly brave steps every woman in that room had taken in order to get where she was. In a business environment that wasn't built for us, we had made our place, then made our marks on the world. I was proud to be among them, and proud to call so many of them friends—Wanda; Christie; Carol; nutrition icon Jenny Craig; Deborah Szekely of the Golden Door and Rancho La Puerta; Ellen Gordon from Tootsie Roll; Muriel Siebert, the first woman to hold a seat on the New York Stock Exchange; clothing maven Josie Natori. There were just so many.

When I was invited to share my own story during "Conversations With . . . ," the supportive environment gave me the courage to open up about something I had not yet publicly acknowledged: MarDell and I had just separated. At the time, I was feeling so shocked, so deeply vulnerable, and so utterly confused, I hesitated to talk about it at all, but I also wanted to be real. I told myself: *If you are going to finally open up about the heartbreak you are feeling, this is the venue to do it in, with women who share a life like yours.*

So, I got up and told my story.

A SHOCKING REVELATION

It happened suddenly, without warning, over breakfast. MarDell announced, unequivocally, that he didn't want to be married anymore. In that moment, my heart broke and my head spun with confusion: *What? How did we get here?*

Now, from a distance, I think I understand it.

MarDell was, by nature, a joyful wanderer who believed in his natural luck, which had been tested many times. He had grown up in abject poverty—in a log cabin in the woods, where he helped hunt for his family's food—but he had clawed his way out with his charm, brains, and penchant for showing up in the right place at the right time.

When he was in the army, his intelligence team was sent on special assignment to Asia. While MarDell was selected to monitor radio transmissions from Manila, the rest of the team went to Vietnam—and all but two were killed. After we married, he entered the aerospace industry, joining Lockheed just as Silicon Valley was heating up. Then, after a chance conversation with a man who had made his fortune in commercial real estate, MarDell abandoned aerospace to pursue real estate development in San Jose. My husband was happiest when he was taking risks. He and his partners developed several properties downtown, and for a while, he was excited by the rise of his business and mine, becoming a noted figure in the region through his own work and as my companion at many charitable and political events.

But it didn't take long for him to tire of Silicon Valley—all the electronics companies and endless tech talk. A Renaissance man, MarDell was always stretching his understanding of the world, always looking at it from new perspectives. The tech world did not offer enough of that, and our engagement with the local arts scene only did so much for him. As his restlessness with the Valley grew, the one thing that seemed to redeem his life here was his close friendship with Bob Noyce, himself a perpetual seeker.

I, on the other hand, was thrilled with my Silicon Valley life—thoroughly immersed in work I loved, engaging in a social scene that excited me, becoming ever more involved in arts and philanthropic organizations, while taking great joy in watching our son, Marc, grow into an intelligent, compassionate, talented teenager. On some level, I was still that young girl who loved to be center stage, and with Casto Travel's success came a giant spotlight, beaming on me. I wanted more of it. I knew MarDell was unhappy, but not the full depth of that unhappiness, and Casto Travel, in a huge expansion phase, took up most of my waking hours.

In his heart, MarDell was Indiana Jones, but there was another side of him: the intelligence agent. He kept certain subjects to himself—and if you asked him about them, he would simply close up. Even so, after Bob Noyce died, I didn't need words to understand that MarDell was coming unmoored. He'd lost his best friend, his co-adventurer. He wasn't sure he wanted to be in real estate development anymore. He didn't know *what* he wanted to do—only that he wanted to be on the move. At one point, he asked me to sell Casto Travel—to pull up my anchor so I could sail the world with him. "We can't do that," I told him. "Marc's whole world is here, and I love my job."

So MarDell set out on his own. He announced that he was going to sail around the Pacific for six months, on his boat, *CASTOWAYS*. I knew he needed it, so I didn't object. Instead, I made arrangements to meet MarDell, with Marc, at various ports of call. I did this to keep our family together, but inadvertently, I taught MarDell that he didn't really need to come home. So, he kept going, the next time hiking across New Guinea, using a local chieftain as a protector and guide as he moved from one back-country cannibal village to the next.

In the end, he did come back, mostly because his partners in the development company needed him. When MarDell had left on his voyage, the firm was doing marginally well; by the time he returned, it was in trouble, and trying to save it was the last thing he wanted to do.

The breakup of the real estate firm, the death of Bob Noyce, and his frustration with Valley life compounded to throw MarDell into an enduring depression. He felt trapped. He sensed—prophetically, it turns out—that time was passing him by. As he saw it, abandoning his current life was the only way to break out. That's why he dropped the bombshell at the breakfast table that morning. It was one of the most traumatic moments of my life. Marc always says that I have the highest emotional intelligence of anyone he's ever met, but I never saw this coming. Perhaps the outside world did, but both Marc and I were completely stunned.

Within six months, MarDell and I were divorced.

When I told my story at the C200 convention, I had none of that insight. The news was still fresh, my feelings raw. I knew I still loved MarDell, and he still loved me, but we had come to a point where we wanted different things. I knew we were forever bonded in our love for Marc and our commitment to put his well-being first as we moved forward. The rest, at that moment, was confusion and heartbreak, and I let it all spill out as I stood at the lectern, looking out across that sea of concerned faces, some nodding, some stricken, some wiping a tear.

When I returned to my seat, I felt emptied out and completely exposed, anxious that I'd gotten too personal, gone too far. As I took a deep breath to settle myself, the next speaker got up and began talking—all business, thoroughly composed—about her silver mines. *Oh God,* I thought, *What have I done? Will they ever invite me back?*

Thankfully, they did, and I learned something important. By sharing my divorce story, I opened the door to connect with other women who'd been divorced, too. The support I received from them gave me hope in the weeks and months ahead.

Lesson: Vulnerability is the foundation of authentic relationships.

For more than thirty years, the friendships I developed through C200 have carried me through all life's ups and downs—and there were plenty of those.

A NEW COMPARTMENT

Recently it occurred to me, with all the extraordinary women I came to know through C200, I never asked any of them to serve on Casto Travel's advisory board. I'm not sure why I didn't ask. It could have been timing. Mine was the generation of women who picked the locks on the doors to the business world and shoved them open. We didn't have ranks of businesswomen up ahead to mentor us as today's generation does. We were all figuring it out together, side by side.

Whether it was conscious or unconscious, when I met the women of C200, I wasn't looking for more business advisers. I already had plenty of those. What I needed—what I didn't even know I needed until I saw it—was friendship with people who understood the life I was living, because they were living it, too. My entire adult life had been segmented into the various roles I played, but when I got together with my C200 friends, I felt whole. We bonded over the challenge of balancing all those compartments—running our businesses, raising children, nurturing our relationships, caring for aging parents, giving back to our communities, and somewhere in between all that, trying to have a little fun. I didn't want to turn these into more business friendships, so I added a new compartment to my life: friendships with women who understood all parts of me. I don't know how I ever managed without them.

Lesson: When distributing your time across the compartments of your life, don't forget to save some for yourself.

CHAPTER 9

NEW TERRITORIES

So many divorces end up with people hating each other—fighting over money, division of property, custody of the kids, or whatever topic fuels their anger. They lose sight of the children, the victims of the adults' decisions. I've never understood that. How can people hate each other after loving each other so much, and loving the children born of their union? Even as we divorced, MarDell and I did everything we could to minimize conflict. We remembered that Marc was our gift to each other, and for both of us, Marc's happiness and success were the most important things. Divorce wasn't the end of our story but the beginning of a new chapter. We stayed closely connected as a family, with our focus now on Marc. MarDell and I went to great lengths to minimize any impact on our son and to give him a normal life.

When we first separated, MarDell took an apartment nearby, but when he began going on his months-long sailing trips, he gave it up. He would take off on his adventures in his boat, and I would fly off with Marc to visit MarDell at various ports. In Tahiti, Marc had his first encounter with a shark; in Hawaii, he swam with dolphins; and in Mexico, he sailed alongside whales. It was a transformative experience for him. On these trips, MarDell and I shared with Marc our love for travel, adventure, and flying. When MarDell finished an adventure, he would come home and stay with us for extended periods. Yes, he was my ex-husband, but he was Marc's father, and I wanted him to be with Marc as much as he could. During these times, he was the most attentive of fathers. I realize not all divorced parents can manage this kind of relationship—many circumstances can get in the way—but I am so grateful MarDell and I could.

In 1991, when Marc turned sixteen, MarDell decided that it was time for him to have a rite-of-passage experience. Of course, being MarDell, this couldn't be just a walk in the park. It had to be a dramatic adventure. Together with two crew members, they would sail *CASTOWAYS* from San Francisco to Hilo, Hawaii, a two-week voyage. Some parents have a difficult time watching their sixteen-year-olds drive off in a car for the first time. Imagine watching your child set sail across the open ocean. *CASTOWAYS* was a forty-eight-foot sailboat with two cabins, which might sound big, but when a vessel like that is carrying your child on a two-week excursion across the Pacific, with no communication, it feels more like a raft made out of toothpicks. I was frantic the whole time, and when they finally called from Hilo, I was so relieved, I jumped on the next available plane to meet them. They had a wonderful trip, but the stories they told—like when a sail broke and Marc had to climb up the mast to help fix it—even today, thinking about it makes me anxious.

EXPLOSIVE GROWTH

As MarDell, Marc, and I settled into a new rhythm together, thanks to the rise of the internet and the dot-com boom, Casto Travel's growth in the 1990s was just as explosive as that of the tech companies and start-ups of the era. The big companies got a whole lot richer and indulged themselves in a luxurious life, including travel and vacations. New ventures sprung up by the thousands, funded with millions of dollars, and their newly minted founder-tycoons imitated their elders. My connection to one of Casto Travel's earliest clients, venture capitalist Eugene Kleiner, had taught me something: when you connect with a venture capital firm like Kleiner Perkins, you become the go-to contractor for all the start-ups they fund. That's why I had placed a Casto Travel office near Sand Hill Road in Palo Alto, ground zero for

VC firms, and set out to connect with VCs like Pitch Johnson, Tim Draper, and Don Valentine.

All those new start-ups, they wanted marketing wizard Regis McKenna, known as the man who put Silicon Valley on the map, for public relations. He and his firm launched some of the most innovative products of the computer age, including the first microprocessor for Intel and the first personal computer for Apple. While Steve Jobs is widely seen as the promotional mastermind behind Apple, Regis McKenna was the real power behind the scenes. He's the one who turned Apple's origin story—a couple of kids tinkering in a garage in Los Altos—into modern-day folklore.

For legal counsel, they wanted Larry Sonsini—Silicon Valley's superstar corporate lawyer and cofounder of Wilson Sonsini Goodrich & Rosati, the law firm that handled the Valley's biggest companies and helped take public many of the most celebrated start-ups. Rumor has it that Larry's offices displayed so many of the Lucite cubes that are awarded for being part of an IPO that, when the 1989 Loma Prieta earthquake hit, Larry's secretary had to duck under her desk to escape injury. For years, his conference table was dented from the falling cubes.

For communications training, new companies wanted persuasion expert Nancy Duarte, founder and CEO of Duarte Design, now the largest communication firm in Silicon Valley, as well as one of the top woman-owned businesses in the area. Nancy developed a unique approach to communications, which applies storytelling and visual-thinking principles to business communications to influence audience behaviors. Now a bestselling author and widely sought-after speaker, she and her team have helped shape the way the world sees brands like Apple, Cisco, Facebook, GE, Google, HP, TED, Twitter, and the World Bank.

For travel, these start-ups funded by the VC firms known for backing winners—they wanted Casto. I can't tell you how many times Regis, Larry, and I ran into each other in the hallways of VC firms or ended up on the same guest lists for IPO celebrations. Nancy and I would see each other at C200 events. Together we formed an unofficial group of outside contractors working for all the hot new companies. Regis himself became a Casto client, and he and his wife, Dianne McKenna, who was a Santa Clara County supervisor, became good friends. For their wedding anniversary, I arranged a special trip to Kenya, where they were given a vow-renewal ceremony officiated by a group of Maasai warriors.

Surfing the ever-swelling wave of our clients' prosperity, by 1995, Casto Travel hit a company milestone that brought with it one of my favorite moments in my career, courtesy of Pitch Johnson and James Treybig. Cowboy Jimmy, as James was nicknamed, was a friendly, laid-back good ol' boy with a brilliant engineering mind. After establishing himself as a computer guru at Hewlett-Packard, he left to start Tandem Computers, with the vision of creating unprecedented computing reliability by essentially bolting two machines together, one taking over when the other faltered. His architecture was quickly in great demand from institutions—newspapers, the military, utilities—that needed that level of reliability.

Jimmy became a Valley legend with his business plan for Tandem. Typically, business plans are mostly fantasy, making predictions for the future based on almost no data—how could they not be, when the company's product (even the market) doesn't yet exist? Despite those limitations, he predicted Tandem's future revenues out five years and hit every number. No one in the Valley had ever done that before, and I'm not sure anyone has since.

Cowboy Jimmy, Tandem, and Tandem's chairman, Pitch Johnson—all Casto clients—were not only a delight to work with but prime examples of the kinds of people who made Silicon Valley feel like a real community. In the spring of 1995, they made a special trip to Casto's office to give me an unexpected award: a framed Tandem memory chip containing 100 million bits to commemorate Casto Travel reaching $100 million in sales. It was such a wonderful, personalized gesture. I wonder how many companies would do that today?

Hitting that milestone was an exciting accomplishment, but plateaus—no matter how high—still didn't interest me. As always, Casto Travel's response was to take full advantage of the boom, growing upward and outward. We borrowed more money, hired more people, and opened more offices. Though I had sworn from the beginning that Casto would remain regional, that we would stick to our core competencies in the Bay Area, changes in the job market and travel industry—not to mention my own ambition—sent me in search of new territory.

WHERE?

During the dot-com boom, we found ourselves sharing a serious problem with our tech neighbors: a shortage of skilled workers. Simply put, we couldn't find new travel agents to recruit in the Valley, nor could we find people willing to move to the region, with its sky-high real estate prices and cost of living—and to pull off our next expansion phase, we were going to need a lot of new people.

Already, Casto Travel had revolutionized the travel industry by migrating some of our services to the internet—the move that got the attention of Harvard Business School. Now we were planning to push the envelope again by opening our own in-house, twenty-four-hour customer service center. Why? Because our greatest demand for special customer service came between midnight and dawn, when we had the least staff available. So, we knew *what* we needed to do, but *where* could we do it?

We needed a welcoming community, an affordable economic climate, and a population of potential talent. We initially looked at Las Cruces, New Mexico, but when word got out, a group of travel agencies in that region banded together and publicly announced that they would use all of the political and social power they had to block us from moving in. Their threats were so outrageous that San Jose's *Mercury News* wrote a story about it. I was incredulous—and even more resolved to find a welcoming community elsewhere.

Fortuitously, a South Dakota senator was visiting Silicon Valley, and—like many state officials trying to capture a bit of the Valley's magic in those days—he put on a lunch to promote economic development in his state, especially its showpiece business sector in Rapid City.

It may sound strange for a company synonymous with Silicon Valley and the fast-moving world of tech to open a facility amid the wheat fields and grazing cows of South Dakota. Frankly, I didn't even know where Rapid City was. But we didn't really have any other options at the moment, so why not give it a shot? To test the waters, we ran a blind ad—a job posting without our company's name or location—in the local newspaper there, and five hundred people responded. That was impressive. So, my HR director and I flew in to check the area out. We were astonished to discover that the airport there was a United Airlines hub and a reservations center for the upper Midwest. So Rapid City had a population of potential hires with prior airline experience, not to mention the local government was anxious to provide incentives—including subsidizing the labor pool—to convince us to set up shop there. That sealed the deal. We established our central reservation system and training department in a ten-thousand-square-foot office space in the Rushmore Business Park.

Up to that point in Casto Travel's history, every new hire went through a process our team lovingly called Casto-izing—learning our company's unique service philosophies and culture. Veteran Casto Travel employees took great pride in mentoring the newbies, showing them the CastoWay. Full Casto-ization usually took about a year, but new hires who didn't begin to adapt within three to six months usually knew themselves that it was time to leave. The Casto Travel culture was not for everybody.

With our new operation in Rapid City, we formalized the Casto-izing process, educating people in our operating principles, which we adapted from Ritz-Carlton: own any problem you encounter and resolve it; recognize we are one team, succeeding or failing together; provide clients with exceptional service from the first hello, throughout their travels, until they reach home; strive for self-improvement in all matters; celebrate successes and praise exceptional service; commit to creating clients for life; operate ethically and professionally, always; add more kindness to the world, every day.

The training center became a crucial part of our business—and remained so, generating talented new employees who arrived on the job fully trained and imbued with the Casto Travel spirit. A month of off-site training there saved us a year of on-the-job training, and that constant supply of new employees gave us an ongoing advantage over other Valley companies that had to fight for every last new hire from a dwindling pool of talent.

Lesson: Don't compete for talent in the same pools as your competitors; look for new pools that you can make your own.

OVERSEAS OPERATIONS

When new airline regulations led to diminishing commissions in the mid-1980s, we repositioned Casto Travel by instituting management fees and transaction fees. By the late 1990s, the domestic per-ticket commission had dropped 20 percent, with a cap of $50 per transaction. Recognizing the airline industry in the United States would never be quite the same again, I wasn't confident that our pricing strategy would be enough to keep us prospering over the long term. So, I went looking for new markets outside the United States with my brother Gus, who had left his position at Intel to join the company as our CFO.

Actually, Gus left Intel for Casto twice, within a matter of days. First, I persuaded him to join Casto because, with all my energy focused on sales, I was not paying close enough attention to the financial side of the business. He resigned from Intel and signed on to help, but after five days in the office, when he fully understood the state of our financial affairs, he said, "Forget it. You're going to go bankrupt. I'm going back to Intel." After a week back at Intel, though, he realized he would always be a small fish in a big pond there; at Casto, he could make a real difference as an integral part of a small leadership team. So, he quit Intel a second time, returned to Casto, and never looked back. Of course, I was elated to have him by my side, especially as we expanded into new markets.

I was especially interested in two locations—India because of the sheer size of the largely undeveloped but technologically astute market, and the Philippines because its travel industry seemed to have figured out a rational pricing model. Both locations presented terrific opportunities, and I knew I could learn something from each of them. In the end, we settled on the Philippines because we already knew the culture, which had Casto-style hospitality embedded in it, and I already had connections, including an ex-boyfriend's cousin, Nonoy Ibazeta, president of a Soriano holding operation that had in its portfolio thirty major companies, including banks, real estate firms, and San Miguel Brewing.

So, when I flew into Manila, in search of opportunity, I met Nonoy for lunch and explained that I was interested in establishing a base for Casto Travel in Manila. He asked, "Why don't you just buy an existing agency here? We have a small one you might be interested in, ANSCOR. We have somebody running it right now, but we might be interested in selling."

I got the impression from Nonoy that the agency was struggling, but I decided to take a look. Sure enough, thanks to poor management, the company had lost most of its customers, and those who remained were unhappy. A lot of people would walk away from a mess like that, but I saw an advantage: we could buy 51 percent of the company's shares for a rock-bottom price. That's how Casto Travel Philippines was established.

In the end, it would take four years, a lot of money, and extraordinary effort to Casto-ize the whole operation, combining the latest advances in technology with traditional hospitality and personalized customer service. Part of that process meant sending Casto Philippines employees to train in our Rapid City facility, which led to some pretty amusing situations, like when twenty people from the Philippines, who had never seen snow in their lives, landed in South Dakota in the dead of winter.

Nonetheless, we had planted our flag in the Philippines. To make sure I had somebody trustworthy in control, I hired my cousin Joe Mantecon, a recently retired executive who had a stellar reputation and a wealth of expertise. In addition to providing travel services for corporate clients in the Philippines, as part of this new venture, we created an accounting center, then added a twenty-four-hour reservation service to complement our Rapid City operations. Once we had established models for ourselves in each of these areas, we began selling those services—and eventually employee training as well—to other travel companies.

Along the way, the pricing model that had attracted me to the Philippines in the first place turned out to be exactly what we needed to thrive outside the United States. I knew the Asian travel industry was leagues ahead of us in the States, but until I got there, I didn't understand exactly why. One key component was a methodology called fee pricing. The airlines presented agencies with a basic price per ticket, then they granted the agencies permission to reprice those tickets for clients, raising the face value enough to cover the agencies' services. Operating like this in the Philippines gave us an advantage over our American competitors. Eventually, we were able to buy the remaining 49 percent of the ANSCOR shares, then the Casto bird was flying solo.

Lesson: Don't enter new markets only to find new sources of revenue; look for opportunities to gain new skills.

In the beginning, Casto Philippines may have seemed a mere sidelight to our nearly $200 million business in Silicon Valley, but in the volatile days ahead, with Marc's initial business plan for Casto Fulfilment Solutions and Gus handling operations there, our Philippines operation would save its big sister in the United States.

MY HEART

As much as planting a flag in the Philippines proved to be an excellent business decision, it held enormous emotional significance for me as well. To return to the country of my birth, to connect with the travel industry in the place where I began my career, to create new job opportunities for people there—I found it all so deeply rewarding. My only regret is that my father—my guardian angel and lifelong champion—wasn't there to see it.

After working at Casto Travel and living with MarDell, Marc, and me for over a decade, in the later part of the 1980s, my father began to show signs of age. Though he was still a real prankster, I could see he was slowing down at work. Maybe he noticed it, too, because he seemed to buck against it. He began flirting with women—harmlessly, of course, just turning his natural charm up a notch, taking joy in the glint in their eyes. No one minded it, and his new energy had the side benefit of making him more attentive to his work and appearance. He was becoming excited with life in a way I hadn't seen since my mother's passing.

Swept up with that energy, he began to assert his independence. After all those years living with us, suddenly he wanted his own place. In our search for an apartment, I made only one stipulation: I wanted him to stay nearby. (I didn't tell him that I wanted to keep an eye on him.) Luckily, we found a spot just down the street from me, and he moved in with his new roommate, a parakeet he named Ralph, who filled the place with song. He told me that, after his long period of mourning, "I'm ready to live."

Every morning, I would stop by his place on the way to the office and knock on his door. He'd open it a crack and peek out, and I would announce, "Okay, Daddy, I want to know exactly what's in your refrigerator."

Why the refrigerator? Remember: I was raised in a sugar family in the Philippines. As the owner of a sugar plantation, my father encouraged sugar consumption—forget what it did to your health; sugar was good for business. When I was young, if he saw me put one teaspoon of sugar in my tea, he'd say, "No, you need more," and dump a few more in. But MarDell was the opposite: he didn't want sugar in the house. Looking back, I can't believe my father put up with that rule. On occasion, he and I would sneak off to get something sweet, but at home, for ten years, he stuck to the rules.

Now that he lived on his own, I was afraid he'd try to make up for lost time, which is exactly what he did: he went sugar crazy. So, I'd stop by, check his fridge, empty out the sugary treats, and replace them with healthy food. Of course, the minute I left, he'd head out to get more ice cream, candy, or pie. It became something of a game. But I couldn't be angry at him. He was having so much fun, and he was so excited about his newly recovered freedom.

About a month after he moved into his apartment, my father, in keeping with his new sense of adventure, decided he wanted to travel, so he and my aunt took a cruise to Mexico. They'd been gone just a couple days when I had received a phone call from Acapulco. It was my aunt: "You have to come down—and hurry. Your father has had an attack."

He had been stricken while they were still at sea, and the moment the ship had docked, my father had been taken by ambulance to the hospital. While my aunt was on the phone with me, my father was on a gurney, gasping for breath, and a surgeon was preparing to give him a tracheotomy.

Desperate to get to Acapulco as fast as we could, my sister and I caught the first flight to Los Angeles. Once we arrived at LAX, I planned to call every client I knew who had access to a private plane or corporate jet—certainly one of them could get us into Mexico faster than a commercial flight could. Until we reached the ground in LA, though, all I could do was pray for my father's safety and will the plane to move faster.

By the time we landed in LA, it was already too late. The gate agent called me and said, "I am so sorry. Your father has passed away."

I couldn't believe it. He was so full of life. How could he be gone? Devastated doesn't begin to describe how I felt. My sister and I, our hearts broken, flew to Acapulco and brought our daddy home. Later, my aunt shared that my father had spent his last night on the ship dancing up a storm with every woman who was willing to partner with him. It gave me solace to know he'd experienced such joy in the final hours of his life.

Our whole family—and my Casto Travel family—came to Daddy's funeral, sending him off by singing "Take Me Out to the Ball Game" as we released balloons to accompany him through his final hole in the clouds. Two weeks later, I received a tourist postcard from Mexico from my father telling me he was having a wonderful time.

My first and most important adviser, I still speak to him in my mind when I'm making tough decisions. I hear his voice, encouraging me and comforting me. Though he died before Casto Travel made its debut in the Philippines, with my whole heart, I believe he was there. Even today, in everything I do, I know my father is by my side.

CHAPTER 10

INTO THE DANGER ZONE

Veteran businesspeople will tell you there is as much danger in growing too fast as in growing too slow. During periods of rapid expansion, when you seem to be living on adrenaline and moving at the speed of light, decision-making processes get truncated, potential problems get overlooked, standards start to slip, and before you know it, you're too far over your skis, about to lose control. Casto was beginning to suffer from all those problems, but we kept speeding forward.

Lesson: Good times require even more attention to the details than bad times.

After all, we told ourselves, these good times might never end, right? We would be fools to stay small and risk getting left behind by more visionary competitors.

Anyway, we seemed to be getting away with it so far, so we kept speeding forward. By 2000, in addition to our operations in the Philippines, Casto Travel had fifteen offices in various regions of the United States, and we had our sights on opening up shop in the UK. We were looking so far into the future, we didn't see the cliff just ahead.

My son, Marc, chose that precipitous moment to make an announcement I never anticipated.

FAMILY BUSINESS

Though I'd welcomed many family members into the Casto Team, I never pressured Marc to join the company. For Marc's part, he'd never mentioned a desire to do so, and his long-time mentor Andy Grove was dead set against the idea. In fact, Andy had strong opinions about many of Marc's decisions.

When Marc was a college student, on a break from studying at Lewis & Clark College, Andy asked him, "What are you studying?"

He replied, "Philosophy."

Andy stared at him a moment, silently, then finally asked, "What the f--- are you going to do with a philosophy degree?" Marc answered with the long spiel he had developed just for this moment. When he finished, Andy asked again, "What the f--- are you going to do with a philosophy degree?"

Marc knew he was defeated, so he told Andy he was minoring in accounting, too. Andy's face brightened: now *that* was something he could work with.

After graduation, Marc worked for a few years at an accounting firm, but the profession just wasn't for him. He took a walkabout trip, backpacking across Europe and into East Africa. At one point, I met up with him in Tel Aviv, and he said, "I want to talk to you about something when I get home."

I was thrilled to find out the "something" he wanted to share was his decision to join Casto Travel. Don't all parents hope their children will carry on their proudest legacies? I was all the more delighted because Marc had come to the decision himself, and not impulsively, but after careful consideration.

In keeping with the Casto philosophy that leaders don't ask their team to do anything they wouldn't do, Marc started learning from the ground up, training like any other employee—accounting, ticketing, reservations, sales—the works. He seemed to enjoy it, but I wouldn't be surprised if he questioned the wisdom of his career choice several times in those early years, because, in 2000, the same year he joined the company, the dot-com bubble burst, pitching Casto Travel into our darkest days yet.

BUSTED

How bad was the 2000 dot-com bust? On March 10, 2000, the tech-heavy Nasdaq index hit a peak of 5,048.62. By November 9, 2000, most internet stocks had declined in value by 75 percent, losing $1.755 trillion in value. By October 4, 2002, the Nasdaq had cratered at 1,139.90, a 76.81 percent drop. Not only did most dot-com stocks tank, but even blue-chip tech companies—Intel, Cisco, Oracle—suffered losses over 80 percent. All around us in Silicon Valley, companies were shuttering their offices. Meanwhile, Casto Travel, which had been riding high in 2000, barreling forward in our global expansion, was suddenly a runaway train without a track.

That's how, soon after the bubble burst, I found myself sitting at the table in our conference room with my brother Gus; my son, Marc; and our lawyer, who'd called the emergency meeting to tell us that the agency was in serious financial trouble. Over a matter of weeks, much of our client list had evaporated, those who remained had canceled all travel, and we were bleeding money. That's when he used a word I had never imagined I'd hear: "You might have to declare *bankruptcy.*"

I was stunned. "Bankruptcy? Where did that come from? We cleared $250 million in sales last year. How could we possibly go bankrupt?"

Gus explained, "Maryles, we're having trouble making collections, even from our biggest and oldest clients. We just can't keep up with all this upheaval, and it's likely to get worse."

I slammed my hands on the table and shouted, "There is no way in hell we're going to go bankrupt. Never! We'll just have to figure out a different solution. We're not going to give up."

Now, a lawyer or consultant may tell you that bankruptcy is, in fact, an intelligent strategy for keeping a business alive by enabling you to hold off creditors and restructure debt. Maybe so, but that doesn't take into account the effect going bankrupt has on employee morale, on the reputation you have with your customers, or on how you are perceived by the public. Most of all, it doesn't consider the effect it has on you, the founder, to accept that you have failed.

I was never going to let Casto Travel go bankrupt. I resolved to fight with everything I had to return the company to solvency, even if it killed me in the process, and it nearly did.

First of all, we put the company on an austerity program, cutting overhead everywhere we could. That program was driven by Marc and Gus, and it wasn't fine surgery—our situation was too dire. It was slash and burn. We closed offices. We went through two brutal layoffs—a miserable experience because we had to let some folks go who had been with the company for years, who truly were like family. It was like ripping off my own arm.

As we battled to survive, we were hit with another blow— several, actually. The attacks on September 11, 2001, the War on Terror, the SARS virus, airline strikes—they caused pandemonium in the travel industry. The shifts happened this quickly: on September 1, 2001, we opened a brand-new office in London, on Victoria Street near Buckingham Palace, with twelve major corporate clients already signed on. Within two weeks, we had lost five of those clients, and the whole UK operation was hanging by a thread.

Eventually, our austerity measures stopped the bleeding, but we didn't have enough cash left to revive the company. I was reduced to begging for help. I swallowed my pride, explained my circumstances to a girlfriend of mine, and asked her for a personal loan. That was doubly humiliating because this wasn't like asking a business colleague to make an investment. I was asking a close friend for a bailout. To my eternal gratitude, she didn't hesitate to help, and I paid her back as soon as I could. In the meantime, that money kept the agency alive.

Within two years, the Valley was showing early signs of recovery. Indeed, thanks to Apple's resurgence, hard-charging companies such as Cisco and Salesforce, and the rise of social networks such as Facebook and Twitter, the region's most prosperous era yet was just about to begin. Once again, we'd made it through the danger zone. Casto Travel—wounded but not mortally—would prevail.

Lesson: When it comes to saving the company, a true entrepreneur never surrenders.

One thing did go well during that awful period. Our investment in Casto Travel Philippines paid off sooner than anyone could have predicted. After 9/11, when flights to and across the United States stopped, we were able to shift our operations to Manila and keep the lights on. If we hadn't opened that office when we did, and where, Casto Travel might have died alongside its Silicon Valley neighbors.

CHILDHOOD JOURNEYS

Though we recovered, by the skin of our teeth, and the Valley would again boom, the first few years of Marc's tenure at Casto Travel proved to be a trial by fire. "Mom," he once confessed, "everything was going so well at the agency—and had been for years—then I came in and everything went crazy. I inherited all of these problems. It took five years of our business going up and down, and up and down again—and all the time not knowing if we were going to make it. I wondered the whole time what I was doing here."

In 2003, San Francisco was beginning to reemerge economically, as were a number of our clients. It was time to get moving. Just as we had after the recession in the 1980s, we moved into acquisition mode while many of our counterparts were for sale at bargain prices.

One agency in particular enchanted me: Rascals in Paradise, in San Francisco. I had worked with its founder, Theresa Detchemendy, at Travel Planners. She was one of those people—she was pure energy. You don't forget Theresa after you meet her. Like me, she got sick of the environment in the Travel Planners' office and said, "I'm out of here. I'm going to go backpacking." I thought, *God, look at your freedom, Theresa—you just get an idea and do it!* Years later, when she started her family, she said, "I'm not going to let this stop me from seeing the world. I'll just take the kids with me and educate them along the way." I loved that about her. That's why she started Rascals in Paradise, packaging family travel to exotic locations. She would organize trips to Africa, setting up classrooms in the wild. She created a trip to Costa Rica to learn about butterflies. In doing this, she built something wholly new: a combination of family vacation, homeschooling, and ecotourism. Having traveled internationally with Marc since he was a seven-month-old taking his first trip to the Philippines, I understood how travel, education, and empathy can go hand in hand. It was a concept I wanted to promote, and Rascals fit neatly with the elaborate trips I was creating for my own clients and their families.

So, I called her and we reconnected. I told her how much I admired her work, and then I asked her if she would be interested in selling her company. Her kids were getting older, she had worked very hard for years, and it turned out, she was ready to take some equity out of her creation. So, we bought the company.

Marc was not very happy about the idea, as there were other opportunities in process that would yield higher returns, most notably the acquisition of a corporate travel competitor in San Francisco, Riser Group. Regardless, he went along with it. Though Rascals in Paradise didn't become a big operation, it was never meant to. What it gave us were some new private clients, a unique supplemental product offering, and Theresa's hard-earned expertise in this emerging field. Eventually, we fully merged the operation into Casto and took pride in offering something exciting to Silicon Valley as it came back to life. Unfortunately, my purchase decision was more emotional than financial—I had fallen in love with Rascals' business model, but ultimately, Riser offered a much better return on our financial and manpower investment.

CHAPTER 11

FOR THE LOVE OF IT ALL

Ask any group of entrepreneurs what they love about launching a business and bringing it to scale, and you'll hear some common answers: the fast-paced action, that "anything is possible" optimism, the flow of inspiration and iteration, the do-or-die stakes behind every decision, the adrenaline rush of risking it all, and, of course, assuming they succeeded, the financial reward. All of that was true for me, too, but I didn't start Casto because I wanted to grow an organization to scale, then sell it. I started Casto because I loved the travel industry. I loved serving my clients with a depth of hospitality they were hard-pressed to find elsewhere. I loved creating once-in-a-lifetime trips that suited their personalities and exceeded their wildest dreams—which was a high bar, since so many of my clients were world-class dreamers. I don't know that I would have stayed on the entrepreneurial roller-coaster ride as long as I did if I didn't also love the business I was in.

Lesson: When you're doing what you love, it doesn't feel like work; it feels like passion.

Andy Grove once said, "Maryles has hospitality embedded in her pores," and it was my great privilege to activate that trait in all aspects of my business, which began with listening to my customers and giving them what they wanted, what they needed, and sometimes more than they ever could have imagined. Every travel agent has a catalog of stand-out stories—quirky client requests, minor missteps, epic saves, and favorite excursions. Following are some of mine.

WOZ

At Casto Travel, we did everything we could to make our customers happy, even when their requests didn't immediately—or ever—make sense. Serving Silicon Valley's notoriously eccentric population, we had more than our fair share of quirky customers on our client list. One of my favorites among them was Apple cofounder Steve Wozniak. In the hard-charging tech world, he stood apart: kind, open, caring, guileless almost to the point of being naïve. He didn't have a mean bone in his body. Forty years later, his success hasn't changed him one bit.

One of Casto's first tasks for Steve was to help him renew his passport. We prepared his papers, and he came to our office to review them. Everything went smoothly until we took the documents up to San Francisco, handed them over to the official at the passport office, and she handed them right back, pointing to Steve's signature and announcing, "This won't do. It has to be his full name."

That's when we noticed how he had signed his name: "Woz."

Now, most clients, when informed of such an issue, would simply redo the documents with a full signature. Not Woz. His response: "Well, Woz is my name." Rather than acquiesce to bureaucracy, he researched passport regulations. Lo and behold, he discovered a rule that said his signature was valid, no matter what he called himself, as long as it was witnessed. With the regulation in hand, we went back to the passport office, and, reluctantly, they agreed that Woz was right. I would venture a guess that his passport still bears the signature "Woz" today.

For all of his gentleness, when Steve believed something should be so, he was relentless until it was so. It was the same with his interests: if he needed to see or know or do something, he became obsessed with it until he had an answer—and as time went on, he had the money and the reputation to do just that. So, when he had an impulse to see the new Legoland in Copenhagen, he dropped everything and booked a trip for his family. In pursuit of his obsessions, be they big or small, Steve would become as excited as a little boy. It was charming, and it kept us on our toes—when Woz called, you never knew what he'd be up to.

On one occasion, he called me and said, "I need to go to London."

I replied, "Okay, for how long?"

"Just for the flight," he said.

I was taken aback. "So, you're flying for twelve hours and then just turning around and flying back."

"Yes. I want to test my new cell phone."

So that's what he did: boarded the flight, landed at Heathrow, made a phone call, and headed back to California. It was crazy, fun, and the stuff of legend all at the same time. Casto Travel kept Steve as a client—business and personal—because he knew we'd keep rising to the occasion, joyfully, no matter how unusual that occasion might be.

IN SEARCH OF MR. PETERS

Mr. Peters coauthored perhaps the most successful business book in history, *In Search of Excellence*, which sold more than five million copies. It was perfectly timed, offering a note of optimism to a nation that was enduring both a deep recession and the depredations of Japanese industrial competition. After it came out in 1982, you were hard-pressed to find a desk in Silicon Valley that didn't display a copy of the book. In the midst of that explosion of interest, Tom hired us to handle his overwhelming travel calendar. He was, it seemed, always on the go. For weeks at a time, he'd travel from city to city, often staying only the day, or at most one night, before heading on to the next.

In order to accommodate the frenetic pace of his speaking tours, Tom wouldn't buy just one plane ticket to his destination, but one ticket for every flight to that destination on his travel day. Apparently, he was concerned that unforeseen circumstances—a speaking engagement that ran long, traffic on the way to the airport, or a canceled flight—would keep him stuck in one city when he was supposed to be delivering a speech in the next. So, if he needed to go from San

Francisco to Boston, and there were seven flights that day from SFO to Logan, we bought him tickets for all of them. If that wasn't enough, on each of those flights, Tom asked us to book two seats, not because he'd have a companion with him but because he valued his alone time. Once he confirmed which flight he was getting on, Janice, who worked at our VIP desk, would cancel the rest.

Does this sound extreme? Consider that, in a matter of weeks, Tom's speaking fee jumped from $10,000 to $100,000 (which would be $250,000 today). Any cancellation fees were a rounding error for a man delivering hundreds of speeches each year.

As you might imagine, all of this frenzied travel took its toll. One day, Tom called Janice and said, "I just got off a plane, and I don't know where I am."

"What do you mean?" she asked.

He said, "I'm in an airport, but I don't know what city I'm in or where I am supposed to go next."

Janice could hear in his voice that he was delirious from lack of sleep. She said, "Stop where you are, Tom." She looked up his travel calendar and told him, "You're in Philadelphia." Then, as all Casto agents learned to do, she went beyond answering the question Tom had asked, and imagined what else he might need: a helping hand.

"Do you have your briefcase, Mr. Peters?" she asked. Thankfully, even in his delirium, he had remembered to take it off the plane. "What do you see around you?"

"I'm near Gate Nine," he said.

"Okay, great," she noted. "I'm going to send someone to find you. Now tell me, what are you wearing?"

Later, Janice told me the whole story: While Tom held on the line, she called airport security, and, like a mother who got separated from her child in a department store, she described our lost client, asking security to locate him and guide him to the airline's club lounge so he could rest. With that arranged, Janice got back on the line with Tom and told him the plan: wait for security, follow their lead, take a nap, then call back for your revised schedule. Once he was revived and back on track with his new itinerary, she asked him to call her upon arrival at his next destination so she could help him get to his hotel.

Lesson: When you encounter a problem, take ownership of it, and see it through to its full resolution.

When people ask, "What makes Casto Travel's service so special?" I think of moments like this—Janice owning the problem, coming up with a creative solution, and supporting the client as she would a beloved family member or friend. That was the essence of Casto hospitality, and it brings to mind something else I loved about my work: there was never a dull moment. When the phone rang, you never knew what awaited you on the other end.

A LOST PASSPORT

After his success at Silicon Graphics, which he had founded, Jim Clark took some of his new fortune and moved up the road from Milpitas to Mountain View, to found Netscape, the company that brought the internet to the masses. I had the Netscape account, and I devoted much of my time to handling Jim's increasingly expensive life—including planning and managing activities at the various destinations Jim traveled to via his private planes.

From one of these excursions, I got a desperate call from Jim. Somehow, on a flight home from an international trip, he had misplaced his passport. Now he was phoning from the plane, en route to the airport in Houston, asking me to furnish a passport before he landed. Immediately, I made an emergency call to the State Department, found the right person, explained who Jim Clark was, and described his real-time predicament. By the time Jim landed, a temporary passport was waiting for him, and he was allowed to reenter the United States.

How did I manage this? Like Silicon Valley, the travel industry is both enormous and, in some ways, a small community. Once you gain the right kind of notoriety, people recognize you and open doors for you. More importantly, if you invest in relationships—show genuine kindness and interest in people—they have a tendency to help you out when you ask, even when your ask seems near impossible. A direct legacy of my mother, kindness is how I operate in the world, which means I created warm relationships not just with people in power but with every gate agent, clerk, administrative assistant—everyone I encountered. The entire Casto Team operated this way. As a result, when clients were stuck in a jam, we had a whole army of people ready to help us get them out.

Lesson: Cultivate your relationships with care. Your success depends upon them.

THE ENIGMA

As a stewardess for Philippine Airlines, more than anything, I loved working in the first-class cabin, where I was assigned to four passengers, and I could focus entirely on creating for them not just a comfortable experience but a delightful one. This required some pretty deft people skills, and over time, I came to pride myself on my ability to read and understand my customers quickly, so by the end of the flight, they felt like I'd known them their entire lives.

I continued to hone those skills at Casto Travel, but every once in a while, I'd meet a client who defied my best efforts to understand them. Ed McCracken was one of those people.

When Ed became chairman of Silicon Graphics, I decided to make an all-out run for the company's business. Pitching to Ed was going to be a challenge: he was extremely bright, he kept his own counsel, and he was a very difficult man to read. But I landed the account. Now I wanted to learn more about my client. What would this company be like under new leadership? I decided the best way to understand SGI's culture was to understand the man in charge. I learned that McCracken was a big proponent of meditation. In fact, he had organized a mindfulness meditation class for his team. So, I joined it. After all, if I could rise to the challenge of helicopter skiing, a meditation class should be a breeze, right?

Wrong.

Before I knew it, I was sitting in a traditional lotus pose, on the floor of an empty SGI office, surrounded by Ed and various other SGI employees. While they dutifully closed their eyes, synchronized their breath, and began chanting a mantra, I kept one eye open, peering around the room, wondering what the hell I'd gotten myself into. I mean, I can't sit still under normal circumstances. Twenty minutes in,

I gave up trying. I untangled my legs from their pretzel position, stood up as quietly as I could, and snuck out the back door. I'd failed in my mission to understand Ed McCracken, but the Casto Team succeeded in keeping SGI happy for years.

A MAN AT PLAY

Al Shugart Jr. played the protagonist in some of Silicon Valley's—and Casto Travel's—greatest success stories and most dramatic cautionary tales. Founder of Shugart Associates, my second corporate client, he helped me build the foundation of my company. Years later, I failed to see the potential of his.

Al's story is so crazy that if you wrote it as a novel, no one would believe it. In its day, Shugart Associates became one of the hottest companies in tech. But the same mix of vision, personality, and skill that made Al a legendary entrepreneur proved to be his downfall. Shugart's product was great, but their production planning and marketing were subpar. Eventually, Al was ousted from the organization he'd built. One of the saddest images in Valley history is that of Al Shugart driving past the Shugart Associates headquarters, seeing his name on the sign, and being barred from entry.

After that great fall, Al bought a fishing boat and worked the lagoon near Candlestick Park. In the mornings, he would stand on the deck, watch the cars driving past on their way to the Valley. After that, he bought a saloon in Santa Cruz and many nights served beer and drinks to young executives who had no idea who he was.

But Al Shugart, if he wasn't a great businessperson, was a genius innovator. As he served those drinks, he was formulating the design for a new kind of small-format disk drive for personal computers. With his idea—and his partner Finis Conner's sterling reputation—the pair landed venture money and founded Seagate Technology in the Santa Cruz Mountains.

I loved Al Shugart. I never forgot how he helped my fledgling company, changing his payables policy to cash on delivery. For as long as he remained at Shugart Associates, I always made it a point to hand-deliver his tickets, and through his good times and bad, he always treated me with kindness and a big heart. Given our long-term relationship, I wasn't surprised when he and Finis called me—together—and said, "We want you to handle Seagate's travel."

They were surprised, however, when I said, "No. You guys are never going to make it."

They laughed out loud.

Honestly, I didn't think they were all that serious about this new venture. I thought they were just goofing around, looking for something to do. Plus, I knew them—they both enjoyed the good life; I thought they'd spend themselves out of business before the company ever got off the ground.

Soon after, when Al called me to book a one-off trip to Paris, he confirmed my hypothesis—he booked first class. During that call, he asked again to hire Casto Travel as Seagate's official contractor, and I again said, "No. Look at what you're doing—you're just getting started, and you know you shouldn't be flying first class, but you're going to do it anyway." Then I added, "Besides, you're all the way up in the Santa Cruz Mountains. I don't want to waste my time driving up there to deliver your tickets."

I'll admit, it was a pretty arrogant thing to say to the CEO of a soon-to-be billion-dollar corporation. But Al got me back. A few months later, when Seagate was going great guns, I called Al and said, "Okay, I'm ready to handle your account. You passed my test. You didn't go broke."

"No," he said.

"What do you mean, no?" I demanded.

"No," said Al, "because you were not there when I wanted you to be there."

Point taken.

Eventually, Al relented, to a degree. Casto handled all of Seagate's Hawaiian sales meetings, but he always held back some of the company's business, just as a reminder that Casto wasn't the only game in town.

Through it all, we knew what we meant to one another, and we remained good friends.

Lesson: Trust in winners—even after they fall, they usually find their way back to the top.

Oh, and by the way, Seagate has dominated the hard drive industry for nearly four decades. I guess I didn't always know my clients better than they knew themselves. But I always tried.

TOP SECRET

In the mid-1980s, soon after Finis Conner left Seagate, I received a call from him. "Meet me at the San Jose Airport," he said. "We're going to have lunch." I'd learned my lesson about saying no to Seagate founders—plus, by now, Finis was a dear friend—so I hopped in my car and drove over to the jet center, to the hangar he'd instructed me to find. There I found two pilots waiting for me. One of them pointed at a private jet and said, "Ms. Casto, we are going to fly you to meet Mr. Conner."

"Where is he?" I asked. They refused to answer.

As it turned out, we were headed about a hundred miles south, to Carmel-by-the-Sea. When we landed, I found a limousine waiting for me, with a driver who would not divulge our destination. So, there I was, sitting in the back of the limo, thinking, *What the hell is Finis doing? Why all the cloak-and-dagger?*

Finally, I was delivered to a restaurant in the seaside town. The minute I laid eyes on Finis, I demanded, "What's with all the secrecy?"

"Well, I wanted to tell you that I'm starting a new venture, Conner Peripherals, and I want you to be my agent."

I was flabbergasted. "That's it? Why didn't you just call me? Why all of this fuss?"

Finis grinned. "Well, I wanted to show you that I'm *big-time* now." He was as excited as a child. So proud to show off his new toys. "It's going to be a billion-dollar company," he told me.

This time, I didn't doubt him.

Conner Peripherals became the fastest-growing company in the United States. By 1990—four years after opening its doors—it exceeded $1.337 billion in sales, the equivalent of nearly $3 billion now. Finis had helped launch two enormous ships, each of which sailed mightily—not bad for the son of an Alabama carpenter. Until the day he retired, he retained his genuine, childlike enthusiasm about it all.

ANNIVERSARY

Back in the mid-1960s, when I landed my first job at that travel agency in Sunnyvale, two things became immediately clear: I hated overhearing my boss's begrudging interactions with his clients, and I loved planning trips for people. Coming off my own bare-bones European honeymoon experience, I spent a lot of time dreaming about what travel should—and shouldn't—be. Later in my career, with Casto Travel's A-list clients, I had the great joy of letting my creativity run wild, on their behalf.

I designed one of my favorite trips of all time for Brad Smith, CEO of Intuit, who sent me an email asking if I'd be interested in planning something special for Alys, his wife. He explained:

> My wife and I will be celebrating our twenty-fifth wedding anniversary. We first met on a blind date in 1991 and were married in 1993. We were set up on a blind date by a mutual friend, and I had purchased tickets to see the Bolshoi ballet when they were in Cleveland, Ohio (where we both lived at the time). As fate would have it, I never made it to pick her up that evening, so we never made it to see the Russian ballet. She forgave me, and we had a great first date (the following week), where I fell in love at first sight.

Brad was a new client, so I asked for a meeting in person. "I need to get to know you," I explained, "before I can start to plan anything." That's how the process always begins—by listening to people's stories, seeing their surroundings, watching for the moments when their eyes light up, and the moments their countenance goes flat.

A few days later, I sat across from Brad in his office and jumped right in: "Tell me what kind of trip you're thinking about."

"Well," he said, "since we never did get to see that Bolshoi ballet performance, all these years later, I'd like to surprise Alys by taking her to see the Russian ballet, only in Russia."

"Okay," I said. "Great. Then let's take her to Russia. She needs to see it right there—and let's make it a secret trip."

He loved the idea, but I was nowhere near done yet.

This was early December. Brad and Elise's anniversary was in April. I knew the Russian ballet was scheduled to do a Christmas performance in San Jose, so with Brad's enthusiastic support, I set up the first step of the "date." Brad's assignment was to bring Alys and their two daughters to the performance. Alys would know they were going somewhere special, but the event itself would remain a surprise until she arrived. Of course, when she realized they were about to see the Russian ballet, she was ecstatic—even more so when Andrew Bales, former executive director of the San Jose Cleveland Ballet, appeared to show them to their seats. She thought that evening's performance was the big surprise.

But after the curtain fell, Brad led a bewildered Alys and their daughters backstage, where they found a smaller stage, surrounded by the dancers they had just watched. On top of that stage sat an enormous, elaborately decorated chair. The prima ballerina approached Alys, took one of her hands while Brad took the other, and together they guided the new, wide-eyed star of the show to that chair.

A troupe of ballerinas followed, carrying a beautiful box, which they laid in Alys's lap. Inside that box, she found a nutcracker, and in its hinged mouth, she found the itinerary for their anniversary trip. I still get chills when I think about it.

As for the trip, Brad and Alys went to Moscow, then by train to Saint Petersburg. She attended a private viewing of the ballet there— twenty-five years and a long way from Cleveland. Along the way, she got to make a Russian doll, she was serenaded by a violinist, she met a host of interesting artists, and she toured the Hermitage and other sites. The whole time I was planning this trip, I kept thinking, *Oh my God, I wish this trip was for me.*

CUSTOM CARE

Fortunately, some of the excursions I planned were for me to enjoy— along with the Silicon Valley power players, clients, and friends I invited as my guests. Often, I would spend months dreaming up all the details, putting them all in place, and only then would I decided who I wanted to invite.

One of these trips took my entourage to the continent of Africa. My special guests there were Mike and Pat Splinter—he was a former Intel executive who became president of Applied Materials, and she also had begun at Intel before becoming a venture capitalist. Also on the trip were Intel's Gerry Parker and Carol Parker, his wife. On the surface, this looked like a tour of the usual stops—wild animal sightings, visits to native villages, shopping. But I gave it a special twist: I recruited Lynne Leakey to be our guide. Lynne had taken the first steps in her career during her brief marriage to Philip Leakey of the family of famed paleoanthropologists. Then she set out on her own, building her reputation as an iconic and beloved naturalist, conservationist, and safari guide. Traveling with Lynne, whose love for Africa ran as deep as her relationships with the locals there, opened doors to experiences and individuals we never would have known without her. Her passion for the preservation of African wildlife was infectious, and the visit she hosted to a camp for elephants orphaned by poaching—it was moving beyond words.

On another trip, to Istanbul, I rented the yacht that Prince Charles always used when vacationing in the region. Our party of fourteen— again, including the Splinters—was tended to by a crew of twenty-one, including a masseuse and a bald hairdresser. As it turned out, having a masseuse was great, but the hairdresser part was not. Somehow, he managed to turn my hair and Pat's orange. But, on a trip like that, it didn't matter; it was all part of the fun. Plus, we learned an important lesson: think twice before entrusting your hair to someone who doesn't have any.

Over the years, I also arranged travel for professional women to attend international conferences. For one, I worked with the American embassy to bring women CEOs from the United States to meet women business leaders in Cuba. We were hosted by Mariela Castro, the daughter of Raul, then president of Cuba. This was a first for our countries, and our meeting covered multiple topics. I was surprised to learn that, for a majority Catholic country, they had open views regarding marriage and divorce, premarital cohabitation, and abortion. All the businesswomen—from the United States and Cuba—bonded over our universal love of children and our families.

Lesson: Success matters only if you pause every once in a while to enjoy it.

You know you're in the right business when your passion for your work follows you into your private life. I've had such fun over the years planning trips for my tribe of women friends. We've been on self-guided walking tours through Spain and Italy, venturing out with a book featuring instructions like, "Walk to the third telephone post, turn left by the creek, and jump over the stream, unless it's too high, then walk farther down, past the large stand of trees, until you reach the sunflower fields, then cross over." As you can imagine, we got lost numerous times, but the wine, paella, spaghetti, and laughter kept us going. We've shared martinis at the Ritz in Madrid, taken tuk-tuk rides through Lisbon in search of street art, been awed by the stunning architecture of the Livraria Lello bookstore in Porto, where J. K. Rowling supposedly got her inspiration for Harry Potter's Hogwarts. One little town we visited in Spain, La Bisbal, so enamored us that we were all ready to buy a place and settle down there. We never did, but eight years later, after our annual trip to Deborah Szekely's Rancho La Puerta in Tecate, Mexico, Las Hermanas, as we call ourselves, are now buying casitas in the new Residences at Rancho development.

Whether I was designing excursions for clients or enjoying an itinerary of my own, everything I did at Casto Travel began and ended with my love of travel. No matter how crazy things got—riding the economic peaks or falling headlong into devastating craters—I never doubted I had chosen the right path.

CHAPTER 12

TRANSITIONS

Just prior to the 2000 bust, our family was rocked by horrible news. MarDell—still out there chasing his next big adventure and dropping down into Silicon Valley between them—began to experience tremors in his hands. The first doctors he visited told him it was likely an essential tremor, a neurological glitch of unknown cause. But as it progressed, MarDell put his engineering brain to work, burying himself in all the available medical research, determined to identify the cause and cure. The search gave him hope, but in time, the tremor proved to be an early symptom of Parkinson's disease. He was just sixty years old. MarDell responded by doubling down on his research, looking for a yet-undiscovered remedy.

The disease progressed slowly but inexorably. As his health began to decline, we knew his adventuring days were coming to an end, so I asked him, "Where do you want to land?" Together, we bought a house in Hawaii, where MarDell felt at home, and Marc and I could easily jump on a plane to visit.

MarDell managed on his own for a while in Hawaii, but as his symptoms became more pronounced, I realized—and Marc agreed— that it was time for me to take over MarDell's care. My sister moved in to help MarDell full-time, but still, I wanted to free up my schedule to travel to the island monthly, so this seemed like the perfect time to hand the keys to the agency over to Marc, to see how he liked being the boss.

Already, he had proven himself capable of the job. Back in 2000, I'd been eyeing a potential acquisition, a bespoke agency in San Francisco, called Holly Travel, that catered to a very high-end clientele. I had decided I wanted to buy it, but first I had to get past the two women who owned it, who were notoriously challenging characters. I decided it was the perfect trial by fire for Marc, who had just joined the company. So, I told him, "You need to figure out how you're going to handle this acquisition. I'm putting it in your hands."

"How should I do it?" he asked. This would be Marc's first real experience closing a deal, and he was understandably nervous, only two weeks into his new job.

"It's up to you to figure it out," I replied.

In the end, Marc closed that deal brilliantly, even at one point walking away from negotiations when they hit a critical impasse. Better yet, it proved a really good buy for us. Years later, he told me, "You really threw me in the deep end. Those two women were *really* hard to deal with. After them, everything else seemed easy."

Six years later, as I freed up my schedule to travel more regularly to Hawaii, I knew Marc was more than ready to take a giant leap forward in a career that ultimately would make him one of the nation's premier travel industry executives. I took great comfort in knowing I now had a successor.

Lesson: An entrepreneur will never be truly successful until he or she has a succession plan.

MarDell passed away on March 9, 2009, just two months after Marc and Julie, his wife, welcomed our granddaughter, Elenora, into the world. MarDell had fought his disease to the end, long enough to meet the first member of our family's next generation. Unknowingly, in his passing, he left us all an extraordinary—and timely—gift.

MARC'S WAY

If you ask me, I'll tell you I handed the reins of the company to Marc in 2006, making him president of Casto Travel. If you ask him, he'll say that "handing over the reins" really meant I reduced my workload by about 5 percent.

Perhaps that is true, at least at the very beginning. I knew he—like anyone—would need time and mentoring to grow into the job, some of which he got from Andy Grove, who never warmed up to the idea of Marc taking over the family business but who hung in there as his cherished adviser just the same.

I also knew having Marc join the company was exactly what I needed. He was my counterbalance: Where I was impulsive, he was measured. When I was reckless, he was conservative. Marc was thorough in assessing opportunities that brought better value to Casto Travel. Moreover, he brought a level of accountability to the company that had not existed before. He converted our company to operate more by disciplines of project management, creating Monday-morning messages and quarterly town hall meetings, and launching Slack for all internal communications. My "cowgirl style" needed to be replaced as Casto was now playing in the big leagues.

I had taken the company as far as I could, and I truly felt that Marc was the right person to take it further. He had a better vision for the improvements and investments we needed to make, from e-commerce to innovation. On sales, he brought a level of professionalism that we desperately needed and won accounts we had no right bidding upon, such as Discovery Communications, our first global win, showcasing our ability to implement and manage global accounts; Flextronics, our largest and most essential win, which kept our business alive; and Electronic Arts, where we established on-site agents and got an insider look at video-game products that inspired the world to play.

Recognizing that Casto operated in the heart of Silicon Valley, Marc understood that we had to be proactive in using new tech products. He initiated Project Moonshot to completely restructure our data management, so we could use predictive analytics to anticipate clients' needs and demands. He introduced Marco Polo, a chatbot with full integration into a booking platform for corporate clients, which offers suggestions based upon prior shopping behavior. Leveraging our close relationships with major airlines, he partnered with them to beta test many of their booking systems. By 2003, Marc had implemented multiple booking systems, with a heavy focus on creating e-commerce opportunities. He also enabled the consolidation of all our servers, networks, switches, and systems into a managed data center, enhancing security and reliability. I did not have the knowledge or experience to implement any of these essential, forward-thinking technologies, but Marc did.

Meanwhile, Marc's sourcing, acquiring, and integrating eight companies into Casto Vacations established the company as a premier agency in this field. Marc then created an independent contractor program for our Vacation teams, which added more revenue and solidified this new division. While we had always been known as a corporate agency, Casto Vacations was now being recognized by tour companies and hotels, winning top awards every year. One of those hotels, the Four Seasons, partnered with Casto, hosting our yearly CAVA (Casto Vacation Agents) awards each year, in a penthouse suite in San Francisco, and providing hotel accommodations for a trip awarded to our Top Vacation Agent of the Year, an award Marc presented, Oscars style.

I'm not going to pretend it was easy, handing the reins over to Marc. His style of management differed from mine, and having a partner again was exceedingly difficult for me. His pushing back on my decisions, or worse yet, my needing to ask him for permission—it was chafing. In my mind, I knew that I needed a successor, but my spirit often rebelled against the idea, much less the action, of deferring to another. For many years, Marc and I tried—and most years, we succeeded—to blend our management styles. When possible, we attempted to insulate the impact of our struggles from the rest of our teams, but rarely were we as successful as we thought ourselves to be.

Though I may have resisted giving up control at times, never did I doubt Marc was the best person for the job. In his years as president, Casto Travel set new company records, approaching $200 million in sales, acquiring three more agencies, and growing our team to nearly three hundred employees across the globe. Better yet, through our travails in the early aughts, together we had learned—we believed—how to recognize early signs of an economic disaster, how to react promptly, and how to move strategically, slashing overhead, closing offices, and conducting selective—yet excruciatingly painful—layoffs.

Surely, when the next downturn came, we thought, with Marc, my brother Gus, and I each acting on our strengths, we'd be big enough, stable enough, and experienced enough to weather it well. So, when the subprime mortgage crisis ratcheted up in 2007, we didn't panic. Marc closed our London operation, which had never been profitable enough, and we focused on continuing to grow our operation in the Philippines. Throughout that year, our tech clients remained largely unscathed. In fact, while unemployment rates were rising around the country, the Valley had added twenty thousand jobs. Even after the stock market crashed in September 2008, in the Valley, the depth of its impact was delayed for several weeks—with businesses and consumers continuing to buy laptops and iPhones—until late October, when the Great Recession hit us like the tsunami that follows an earthquake. Then we learned that you just can't prepare enough for a once-in-a-lifetime event.

Everywhere we looked, tech giants were cutting their workforces, and start-ups were boarding up, leaving no forwarding address. The streets normally jammed with traffic fell quiet, and the Valley's perpetual motion seemed to stop dead in its tracks. In the fray of it all, any company that managed to keep its lights on immediately suspended all business travel. Two-thirds of our clients dropped off our rolls, and our sales evaporated overnight.

This was different than 2001, when dot-coms fell victim to their own hype, but nationwide corporate, government, and consumer spending on telecom and computer equipment remained high, allowing for a relatively quick recovery. This time, all sales channels were hit—by declining housing values, credit freezes, and the crisis on Wall Street—and the Valley buckled.

At Casto, we quickly realized our 2001 austerity strategies wouldn't be near enough to get us through to 2009. Once again, we were forced to resort to layoffs—three rounds of them, this time managed by Marc, who took over nearly all terminations. We shut down branch offices, dropped several acquisitions—including Rascals in Paradise—and cut loose entire departments. It was a devastating time, a nightmare that lasted nearly three years. We had all worked so long and so hard, we had made so many sacrifices, we had come through them all as one big extended family, and now it was all crashing down around us. Before long, we found ourselves scrambling every two weeks to make payroll.

The absolute nadir came in 2009. We were not only out of money but in the red. Our creditors were calling in their notes. We were $100,000 short of making payroll. We were within days of closing our doors. Then, MarDell—months after his death—gave us his last gift. That same week, his life insurance policy paid out, and we were able to cover the payroll shortfall.

In that moment, I had no doubt: MarDell was watching over Marc and me. He had supported me as I'd started this career path. He had believed in me—sometimes even more than I had believed in myself—as I'd built the Casto ship and steered it through all kinds of water. He had celebrated my successes, and even when my work consumed me, he understood it was my passion and accepted that I needed to keep following my dreams, even when it meant separating so he could follow his. Now, at Casto Travel's most desperate moment, he gave me, and Marc, a second chance.

CHAPTER 13

THE CASTO FAMILY

There's an old saying: "Fall down seven times; get up eight." That's all you need to do to win: keep getting up. Through a combination of skill, luck, and an amazing team, by the end of 2010, Casto Travel, once again, had gotten back up.

Looking back across that decade, I am so proud of Marc. He had joined the company as a young professional with a few years' accounting experience, just in time to watch us fall from an unprecedented high into the 2001 recession. Now he was closing out the decade as a husband, a father, and a seasoned business leader, having steered Casto Travel out of an even bigger storm, on course toward renewed prosperity.

The travel industry has recognized Marc's numerous contributions by inviting him to join the board and act as chair of the Commonwealth Business Travel Group, a select group of the most influential travel management companies; by welcoming him to the board of the American Society of Travel Advisors (ASTA) to serve as vice chair, making multiple presentations on Capitol Hill; and by honoring him as a Global Business Travel Association Ladders program's Mentor of the Year.

Running a family business has its rewards and challenges, and I have experienced both, with my brother Gus as the Casto Philippines president and Marc as the Casto US president. Being in the middle of it all was like watching a tennis tournament, not knowing where the ball was going to land. Both good players, Marc and Gus made sure the ball was never on the ground for long. Was I frustrated at times? Absolutely, to the point of wanting just to pack it all in. Was I elated when things were going right? Yes, and those times felt like *Dancing with the Stars*, with both Marc and Gus as my partners. For all our years together, I would not trade any of what we have gone through, as each of us in our own ways made Casto the company it was and still is.

They aren't for the faint of heart, those precipitous ups and downs, and no one gets through them alone. Marc, Gus, and I had each other to lean on, but what truly enables a company to right its course is the hard work of a fiercely dedicated team.

THE CASTOWAY

From the beginning, the secret to our company's success—its growth, grit, and survival against the odds—has always been the people of Casto Travel, each and every one of them. To Casto-ites, hard work and superior customer care was a religion. Their commitment to clients, their willingness to go the extra mile, their kindness, creativity, and generosity—boom or bust, Casto Travel employees brought their full selves to work, night and day. They never clocked out early. They never even looked at the clock. They kept going until their own work was done, then looked around to see if anyone else needed help. On top of all that, they earned us a reputation as "the fun company." Somehow, amid all the intensity of the job, we seemed always to be up to some shenanigans. I remember receiving a call from a client one day, asking, "Why is one of your salespeople walking around our campus in a chicken costume?" I told the truth: "It's costume day." What else was I going to say? It was an impressive costume, too—full body, feathers, wings, and everything.

Even when we were facing our greatest challenges, the Casto Team's efforts never waned, and client satisfaction never dipped. It wasn't as if they didn't understand what we were facing. When trouble hit, I was always open about it, but in understanding our troubles, the team only buckled down and worked even harder—this was their company, too, and they would do anything to help it survive. It wasn't just about the money for them—goodness knows if they were only looking for a paycheck, they would have jumped ship at the first sign of choppy water. They truly cared about the company. About the clients. About each other.

Was I responsible for this morale and commitment? No. I invested in the development of our team—their job skills and their personal growth. I respected them as professionals, giving them the leeway to use their natural talents and creativity in service of our clients. Then I got out of their way. I put my trust into the Casto family, and they returned it tenfold. Marc codified our CastoWays in his release and promotion of "10 Commandments of Casto" and "10 Key Values of Casto."

Four extraordinary employees exemplify just what it meant to be a Casto-ite.

Magda Alarcon joined Casto soon after it was founded and stayed thirty-eight years. She was our Travel Goddess. Her Rolodex held the contact information for every Who's Who in the travel industry, and she was a bulldog when it came to meeting our customers' needs.

When pitching our concierge services—a membership-only offering—to VC firm U.S. Ventures, Magda and I were receiving an icy reception from one particular executive admin. Finally, after much coaxing, she relented, saying, "Okay, fine. I'll give you a test. I'm not getting anywhere trying to book a table for four at French Laundry this Saturday. I've been trying for the last month, with no luck."

Apparently, her boss had invited people to dinner at the legendary restaurant crowned with three Michelin stars, without first procuring a reservation—which people typically booked up to six months in advance.

Magda calmly replied, "No problem, we'll handle it."

That was the Casto Travel bible on full display: *No is not an option. We always say yes.* I walked out of that meeting with absolutely no idea how Magda would pull this off. Well, she did it, calling nonstop every hour, every day. By Thursday, French Laundry called Magda to tell her they'd had a cancellation. The U.S. Ventures party was in, and the company signed on for our concierge services.

Marian Wuertz saved Fred Hartman's family vacation. A client from Oak Investment, he had booked a tour for his family that would begin in Lima, Peru, the day after they were scheduled to arrive in the country. Unfortunately, their originating flight from San Francisco to Houston was delayed, so the Hartman clan seemed destined to miss their connecting flight to Peru, and with it, the start of their tour. Fred Hartman called our after-hours line, and Marian sprang into action. She called United Airlines, found out the gate number for the Houston-to-Peru flight, then called the gate agent at the Houston airport and convinced her to delay the connecting flight until the Hartmans arrived. Then, she arranged for a United rep to meet the family at their arrival gate and to transport them to the connecting flight.

The family made it to Peru on schedule, and Casto Travel had a client for life.

Eileen Young took an early-Saturday-morning call from an after-hours agent, informing her that one of her clients needed her attention ASAP. Eileen phoned the client immediately and learned that he had run out of the office at C-Cube on Friday night, without picking up his plane ticket from the company's on-site Casto office. His flight was leaving early the next morning, and he couldn't make it back to the office to pick up his ticket because he was booked all day with parenting duties.

He asked Eileen if she could drive to C-Cube, pick up his ticket, and deliver it to his house in Los Altos. Without any hesitation, she jumped in her car, drove ten miles in one direction to C-Cube in Milpitas, then drove twenty miles in the other direction to deliver the ticket.

On another occasion, one of Eileen's clients had arrived in San Jose, rushed to his car, and was driving to a meeting when he realized that he had left his laptop in the seat pocket on the plane. Eileen called American Airlines, found out the client's arrival gate, got the number of the San Jose Airport ticket counter, got the counter to transfer her to a gate agent, then talked the gate agent into boarding the plane and retrieving the client's laptop, which was waiting for the happy traveler as he exited his meeting.

Lynn Dorner joined Casto as an agent in 2003 when we acquired a small firm in Mountain View, then rose to the ranks of director of operations and vice president. In that role, Lynn and our VP of sales, Frances Mincey, attended a meeting with a long-term client, Harmonic, where they learned the company's newly hired VP of human resources wanted to bring the travel contractor from his previous employer with him.

With no hesitation, Lynn and Frances offered to install an on-site Casto agent at the company the very next day. Then, knowing how important it was to keep the account, Lynn—who, like all Casto leaders, kept up her agent skills—packed her Casto bag and moved to a desk at Harmonic, staying on-site for months to ensure that we kept the account.

As VP of operations, Lynn oversaw Casto's Visa and Passport Department, so she gained in-depth knowledge of regulations and requirements. She even visited consulates in SFO to develop friendly relationships with the personnel there.

Occasionally, due to jurisdictional requirements, we had to process visas through a network of affiliates around the country. Once, we had a Casto client who needed a visa that could only be processed in Washington, DC. Due to a holdup at the DC embassy, the visa had not arrived in San Jose in time for him to begin the first leg of his journey.

Lynn's reaction? She boarded a red-eye to DC, rented a car there, drove to the consulate, picked up the paperwork, returned to Dulles Airport, met the client at his departure gate, and handed him his passport and visa just as he departed for Europe. She then headed to her departure gate and flew right back to San Jose.

How could we not succeed with people like these on the Casto Team? They were nothing short of inspiring.

Of course, these superstars could operate this way only because other Casto-ites had their backs. That was a critical tenet of our culture: whenever a need arose, whatever your job, you stepped in to help, and if you were a manager, you asked nothing of your team that you weren't willing to do yourself, which included assuming other employees' duties while they rushed off to deal with an emergency. At Casto, we made it possible for each other to accomplish the impossible.

Even in the heart of Silicon Valley, the tech capital of the world, people are the real key to success. I've watched so many firms replace people with technology, hoping to increase profits or save a buck. But technology will fail them eventually, because technology doesn't care.

People care, and that caring drives their efforts. *People* have passion, and sometimes only that passion will get you through.

In our darkest days at Casto, nothing and nobody could break our spirit. That spirit endures today. I've heard former employees say, "Once you're a Casto, you're always a Casto." I find that so gratifying because I know they aren't talking about my influence but the powerful culture *they* created. I merely built the stage on which they performed their magic.

Former Casto-ites still regularly get together. As I write this, just yesterday, I was on the phone with five of them, sharing stories—all the birthdays, weddings, and new babies we celebrated; the divorces and deaths we mourned together; and all the crazy moments in between— like the times I went racing around Rapid City, clinging to the back of a team member's motorcycle. These stories remind us that Casto Travel wasn't a mythical place. It was real, and we built it—all of us—together. When Casto-ites left the company, they took that culture with them. I like to think of them seeding it in their next places of employment, growing Casto-style dedication, ingenuity, hospitality, and kindness in new territories around the world.

Business theorists sometimes talk about a company as family; this is what one looked like.

CHAPTER 14

LETTING GO

Andy Grove always said, "Maryles, you have two children. You have Marc, and you have Casto Travel." By 2010, my first baby had grown from its two-room office in Los Altos to a regional powerhouse to a national, then global, presence, keeping pace—and staying relevant—alongside the travel industry's fundamental transformation. Even so, with the relationships between the airlines, agencies, and customers changing, perpetually and rapidly, we knew we'd need to do something more. Two words floated in the back of my mind: "exit strategy."

We needed a plan for Casto Travel, one that would reward everyone for their hard work and loyalty over the years. Maybe it was time to think about selling.

In fact, we had already been approached by a potential buyer once, back in 1995. Remember Rosenbluth Travel, that firm that took over the corporate work at Intel? Well, in the years that followed, I became friends with Hal Rosenbluth, which made our "co-opetition" much easier. In dealing with the often difficult and demanding Intel purchasing and accounting departments, Rosenbluth came to appreciate just how good Casto Travel really was. So, he approached us with an acquisition offer.

The fact that we had a corporate suitor was gratifying, but it felt too early. We were still having a great time, growing rapidly, and exploring new ideas. Still, curiosity got the best of me, so I went through the motions, figuring out my bottom line selling price and setting up negotiation meetings.

Marc was still in college at the time, but I flew him down to join in those discussions with my brother Gus and me—after all, the outcome would affect him as much as anyone. The Rosenbluth team made us an opening offer that was just three-quarters of our minimum, and not much more than half of our own opening position. We were too far apart, and no amount of pushing got us close enough. We departed on amicable terms.

The negotiations with Rosenbluth may have fallen apart, but it did leave me with something. I now knew the price I wanted for Casto Travel—and through the good and bad times to come, I never deviated from it.

Lesson: Determine your value, then refuse to settle for anything less.

Roll forward twenty years and, now veterans of many wars, facing an uncertain future in a rapidly changing industry, we decided it was time to aggressively pursue a buyer. Andy Grove was heavily involved as an adviser to Casto Travel then, meeting Marc for lunch in Palo Alto every two weeks to discuss company operations. When Marc mentioned seeking a buyer, Andy prevailed upon him the necessity of selling Casto. His argument: we had a dying business model in an increasingly obsolete industry, and the company would never again be so valuable. But Andy had another motive: he wanted Marc to move on to bigger things, and he believed Marc's commitment to me was holding him back. In his usual blunt way, Andy said, "Your worst attribute is your loyalty to your mom. You need to get out." (Said the man who called his mother every single day until the end of her life.)

So, in 2015, when we received an offer from a large travel firm in Omaha, we jumped on it. Marc met with them and arranged for the principals to fly out to San Jose to meet me. Then I flew to Omaha to meet their staff. Then they made an offer lower than the one we got in 1995. Andy insisted we take it. He was convinced it was our best—and probably only—chance to find a buyer. As far as he was concerned—and Marc with him—the deal was as good as signed.

But in meeting the men in San Jose, I got a bad feeling. They were good guys and good businessmen, but culturally, they were true

Midwesterners. I knew they would never make it in Silicon Valley, and when they inevitably failed, all that I was trying to secure for our employees—stock, health care, job security—would be lost.

So, we had a problem: Andy and Marc assumed that the acquisition was as good as complete, and I felt sick when I thought about agreeing to the deal.

In fact, that was my order: I was to call the CEO of the Omaha firm and say, "Okay, it's a deal." But as I dialed the phone, it hit me: I couldn't do it, and when the CEO answered my call, that's what I said. After I hung up, I went next door to Marc's office and said, "Marc, I just told them no." He was shocked—and disappointed—but in the end, he understood and supported me in my decision.

Andy, on the other hand, was appalled—and furious. He nearly choked when I told him, then shouted, "How could you have done this? Your son will never leave the company as long as you are there!"

Four years later, we were again approached, this time by a large international travel firm, Flight Centre Travel Group, headquartered in Australia. Throughout those years, Casto had been approached by multiple interested parties, but Marc did not consider the offers, as he did not feel they were the right partners for us. Flight Centre was different. Marc shrewdly understood the value of this acquisition and advised me about the seriousness of this offer, sitting me down and asking me to set my drop-dead price. I gave him the number I had decided on all those years before.

"Okay," said Marc. "Now I know. I can negotiate any number higher than that."

In the end, he did just that. The number he negotiated exceeded my expectations, and I was very happy for it.

Flight Centre had been started as a tour bus operation in the UK by a couple of twenty-three-year-old Australians with no business education—an idea they'd hatched over a pint in a Munich beer hall. In 1982, they moved to Brisbane and started again, eventually growing Flight Centre to be the largest company in Australia. At the time of our negotiations, they had nineteen thousand employees in eighty countries, and annual revenues of $1.25 billion. That sounded pretty solid to me, but facts and figures are one thing, the character of a company is something altogether different, and that's what I needed to see. In particular, I wanted to meet the founder and CEO, Graham Turner.

A month after the sale, Marc and I flew to Brisbane. Arriving at Flight Centre's headquarters, what I saw was better than I could have hoped. It was as if we were back home in Silicon Valley, in the headquarters of Google or Facebook: the same casual intensity, a sense of purpose mixed with an air of play. I remember thinking, *This is Marc's new company. It's perfect.*

Then it got better. Graham—"call me Skroo, it's my nickname"—Turner appeared at the top of the staircase, spotted us, and came running down. He thrust out his hand in a wide-open Aussie greeting, but I said, "I didn't come all the way here to shake your hand. I want to give you a hug."

We had a great time that day, especially at dinner. We chatted for a long time about our respective careers, the histories of our companies, and our—thankfully—aligned business philosophies. Like most businesspeople, Skroo was curious about Silicon Valley and all its notorious characters. I didn't disabuse him of his vision of the place or its personalities.

I returned to the Valley, comforted in the knowledge that we had found the right buyer to take Casto Travel into its next era. I was only sad that Andy Grove didn't live to see Marc's triumph.

END OF AN ERA

Beginning in 1980, I got involved with community nonprofits and charitable organizations. It was part of my upbringing and my faith to help improve my community, not to mention it became the backbone of my social life. The first big initiative I joined in on, along with Karen Loewenstern, Anita Del Grande, and Phyllis Romine, was to convince the struggling Cleveland Ballet to spend half of its season in Silicon Valley, thus establishing the San Jose Cleveland Ballet.

As I stretched my involvement to other nonprofits, Andy Grove sat me down and gave me one of his most important pieces of advice:

A CEO should never sit on the board of directors of another company or of a nonprofit. Your job is to devote every waking hour to making your own company a success. That is your only job—and you owe it to your people. If you want to do charity work, do it as a volunteer or an adviser, and only for a predetermined interval. Otherwise, you will end up dividing your time and your loyalties.

I followed Andy's rule, mostly, then I added my own twist: when I finally did start joining nonprofit boards, I would serve only for two or three years, then transition out so someone with fresh energy could come in. That had the added benefit of allowing me to get to know many different organizations, inside and out, including the San Jose Rep Theatre, the San José Museum of Art, and El Camino Hospital. Later, after I purchased an apartment in San Francisco, I joined the board of the San Francisco Exploratorium and the San Francisco Commonwealth Club, where Gloria Duffy, president and CEO, and I started the funding campaign for their new building on the Embarcadero.

The fact is that you never really know the community you live in if you just stick to your career. Volunteering in nonprofit, education, and arts organizations, you really feel the pulse of your town, learning where it is healthy, where it is weak, and where you can contribute the most not just to the quality of your own life but to that of your neighbors and employees.

One nonprofit board that I joined—and stayed involved in beyond my typical tenure—even Andy understood: the Parkinson's Institute.

I first became involved when MarDell got sick, and I continued with them because their work is so important. I have met some of the most remarkable and inspiring people at the institute, who fight to live their best lives, even in the face of their declining health. I'll never forget the heart-wrenching sight of Muhammad Ali shuffling into an institute event on the arm of his wife—this huge, powerful man rendered helpless, barely able to talk, but showing up anyway. The Institute collaborated on a number of projects with Michael J. Fox, who was diagnosed so young, and who has somehow managed both to keep his career alive and to use his celebrity to raise awareness and funds to fight for a cure.

Through my volunteer work there, I learned about the full nature of Parkinson's Disease, and one particular detail stood out to me: it can cause radical shifts in attitude and behavior. Looking back, I wondered if that had contributed to MarDell's sudden impulse to cut ties with the Valley—and upend life as we knew it—to sail off for destinations unknown.

My understanding of Parkinson's would lead to another insight, this time about my dear friend Andy.

After Andy retired from his CEO role at Intel, he shocked the business world by announcing that he had prostate cancer. In typical Grove style, he immediately set to work giving himself a PhD in the subject, dedicating himself to finding a cure, generously sharing his knowledge, and publicly encouraging men over fifty to get screened for the disease.

Marc and I often had dinner with Andy and Eva during this period. Though I had noted a change in Andy's appearance, I assumed that it was the result of his cancer treatment. But then, one evening, I looked at Andy's face and notice something sadly familiar. I blurted out, "You have Parkinson's!"

Without a word, Andy looked me directly in the eye and nodded.

Soon after, he went public with that news, too. Like the lion he was, he threw everything he had into his own treatments and the race for a cure, for each of those deadly diseases. Even as the Parkinson's took an ever-greater toll on his health, Andy refused to deny its cost, or to hide from the public eye. It was one of the most heroic things I've ever seen. Andy had never given an inch to failure; he wasn't going to surrender now, or to hide from the truth. Remarkably, his mind was never affected by the disease—in his last days, his intellect was formidable, his attitude ferocious, and he was still twice the business strategist of anyone else in America.

He died on March 21, 2016. His influence on my family, our company, the Valley, and throughout the world—it has been incalculable, and I miss him dearly.

I can't help wondering how our conversation would have gone if I'd had the chance to tell him about Casto Travel's acquisition by Flight Centre. Probably something like this:

I'd say, "See? I told you I knew what I was doing."

He'd say, "Okay. I guess you did."

But in the end, Marc did what Andy had always hoped he'd do: he left the Casto nest, taking flight toward bigger things. In June 2020, Flight Centre named Marc president of its leisure brands, America division. So, in that sense, I suppose Andy and I both won this time: Andy's wish came true, and I could not be prouder of my son.

During his tenure as Casto's president, Marc kept Casto Travel's values in place while expanding the operation into one of the top travel management companies in the nation. As people say, timing is every-thing, and Marc's timing in facilitating the sale of Casto USA, before COVID-19 hit, was a gift he gave to me and our family.

CHAPTER 15

FULL CIRCLE

As part of the Flight Centre deal, I retained ownership of Casto Travel Philippines. So instead of retiring, I'm busier than ever, traveling back and forth between California and the Philippines, or hosting Zoom calls from my home in San Jose. The operation there now has more employees than Casto Travel ever had, but instead of serving travelers, we have moved into the travel support industry, providing a broad menu of services to travel agencies, from call center support to technical assistance to accounting to data analytics to customer care training. In an amusing turnaround, Flight Centre has signed on as a client.

Like everyone else in the travel industry, Casto Travel Philippines has been hit hard by the pandemic, as has Flight Centre. The original Casto Travel still survives inside its new parent operation, but like the rest of Flight Centre, it has suffered layoffs. I have no doubt that if we hadn't sold when we did, the agency would never have made it through 2020. But I'm optimistic about the future of our Philippines operation.

One of my favorite offerings of ours is Casto University, a comprehensive training program for upcoming travel professionals. I always said I wanted Casto Travel to become the Harvard University of customer care training, and that's what we're doing in the Philippines. There it's hard to get hired as a travel adviser unless you already have experience. So, Casto University creates opportunities for people with little to no experience to learn geography, the airline computer system, and travel agency responsibilities while developing Casto-level customer care skills.

I hope Casto University graduates will learn what I did: You don't necessarily need to earn a degree from a fancy school to succeed in life. You need determination, energy, focus, and grit. You need to commit to making *life* your university—to learning everything you can from the situation you're in, then making the most out of those experiences everywhere you go.

When I entered Philippine Airlines' stewardess training program, I didn't realize I was building the foundation for an entrepreneur's life. But the professionalism and people skills that I began developing there became the quality that set Casto Travel apart. When I failed horribly as an Avon Lady, I still took the sales training MarDell had given me and used it to get Casto Travel off the ground. When I found myself stuck in that first travel agency in Sunnyvale, making a mental list of the customer service crimes my boss committed on a regular basis, I didn't know I was developing my service standards for the future Casto Travel, but I was. Similarly, the less-than-optimal employment conditions I experienced at Travel Planners sparked my vision for the culture I wanted to create with my own team one day.

No matter what position I found myself in, I took seriously any training I received so I could excel in my job, but the learning didn't stop there: I watched everything that happened around me, noticing what worked and what didn't, what propelled success and what stymied growth. Then I put those lessons to work for me. Anyone can do this—a barista at Starbucks, a cashier at a grocery store, a teacher's aide at a preschool—wherever your work begins, you can start building a powerful skill set that you'll take with you as you grow.

Lesson: No matter where you start, learn everything you can in that position, then leverage those lessons to help you grow.

NEW LIFE

In 2009, when my granddaughter Elenora was born, Julie and Marc gave me the greatest gift: inviting me, along with Julie's mom, into the room to witness the birth of a new generation. Two years later, they doubled my joy when they welcomed Abigail into the family. Ele and Abi are my pride and joy, and Julie is an absolute treasure. A sixth-grade teacher until she retired to focus on raising the girls, Julie is a talented artist whose paintings and murals have graced the walls of offices and homes in the Valley, including Casto offices, over the years, and her involvement as vice chair of the Mexican Heritage Plaza had a real impact on that community. I adore her, and I love every minute I get to share with those girls.

Once, my granddaughters were over at my house and we were all in our pajamas when I asked if they'd like to drive over to the Casto office to say good night to their dad. They loved the idea—so, still in pajamas, we jumped into my car and headed to Casto Travel headquarters, a few miles away. As we drove up, Abi noticed—perhaps for the first time—the brightly lit sign out front. She carefully read the letters: "C, A, S, T, O. Grandma!" she shouted with glee. "That's our name!"

I flashed back to that moment when Marc was an infant, I had just dissolved my business partnership with Lee, and my tiny team of employees sat around our half-empty office space, brainstorming names for our new company. They suggested "Casto Travel," and before I would agree, I told them, "You have to remember, that's Marc's name. If we do this, we all need to promise that our work will give that name the honor it deserves."

Hearing those letters ring out in Abi's singsong four-year-old voice that night—it brought tears to my eyes, along with a wave of gratitude for those original Casto-ites—and every member of the Casto team who followed—for living up to that promise.

Speaking of our name, years ago, when the Casto logo was ready for an upgrade, one of the designers said to me, "You know, your bird doesn't have to be trapped in the *A* of your business name anymore. You can set it free." The symbolism had never crossed my mind. I had always seen myself as just one among many employees, embedded in the company, struggling to lift us off the ground. Now I realized that I *had* been successful—I had weathered all the good times and bad. I had escaped all the cages I had found myself in. I really was *free*. After that redesign, an elegant set of wings hugged the *O* at the end of our name, as if soaring above the globe.

More recently, looking toward the next iteration of Casto Travel, we needed another image refresh. This time, I asked the newest generation of Castos to help me decide where we should place the bird. Thanks to Abi and Ele, on today's Casto Travel logo, the *V* opens into an expansive set of wings, big enough to lift the whole company off the ground. This dynamic and talented duo have also now designed Casto University's logo, and at the rate they are going, my "gratis" status will soon end as demand for their talent goes viral.

Abi is eleven years old as I write this, Ele thirteen. Both Casto girls have become avid wanderers for their love of travel. They've taken trips to The Philippines, Thailand, Mexico, the Panama Canal, Galapagos, and they're just getting started. I can't help but think about the grandfather MarDell could have been to them—he'd have them out sailing on the *CASTOWAYS* for sure. He's certainly present in their adventurous spirits.

Who knows what the future will bring, but right now, Elenora plans to study astrophysics to research the galaxy—another Casto looking toward the sky—and Abi wants to create the biggest library in the world so everyone can have a book to read. They might have to settle for exploring the East Coast for a while, though, because along with Marc's promotion came a relocation to Flight Centre's Boston office. He and Julie bought a home outside the city where the girls can be as free to roam outdoors as I was on my family's farm growing up. Of course, I don't want to miss out on that, so I plan to join them.

Will I miss the Valley? Of course. It's been my home for fifty-five years. I will always love how it pulses with entrepreneurial energy, attracting dreamers intent on becoming the world's next icon. That said, the Valley isn't the same place it used to be. For all that's been gained since those early days, something important has been lost—the wild, raw edge of it. The great pioneers of tech, the men and women of singular character and bold risks, are all but gone, replaced by a new and, to me, less familiar crowd. That original cast of characters—arrogant and humble, charismatic and opaque, genius and troubled, cantankerous and kind—formed a community unique in history, where an unemployed stewardess from the Philippines could stumble into an entry-level job in a travel agency and transform herself into a successful entrepreneur.

I'm sure I'll come back to the Valley in the winters, when the snow falls in Boston, but I'm also looking forward to a new adventure. My father always told me to look for that hole in the clouds. Well, playing with my grandchildren in Massachusetts while running my company from the other side of the world, an entrepreneur-grandmother—I've found my next hole in the clouds, and I'm about to fly through it.

ACKNOWLEDGMENTS

This book began as a team effort from the very start. It began while playing dominoes in the backyard of my San Jose home with Joe DiNucci (who still needs to win). Thank you to Joe and Atiya Dwyer, my publishers at Silicon Valley Press; to Brenna Bolger of PRxDigital; and to Mike Malone, a friend and Valley historian, who knew the original cast of characters; and Cheryl Dumesnil, who both lovingly brought this book to life. You made it possible for me to write this story.

To my son, Marc, for remembering many things I had forgotten; being at my side; supporting something great, outrageous, brilliant, disastrous, wacky. Because, why not? We can make decisions together or alone. You have my gratitude, always.

To Gus, from starting our journey to the many different paths taken to reach the other side; Miel, Ella, Carla, and Julie, I stand in admiration of you. To my traveling girlfriends, Mary Huss, Judy Koch, Connie Martinez, and CW: we have a travel book adventure in the making. To Max and Lulu, my added grandchildren. To the people inside the pages in this book for the patience, guidance, mentoring, and for giving me the wings to fly. You are in my heart.

And a special tribute to the gifted photographer George Wedding for the book cover. He had the vision twenty-one years ago of dragging an old desk inside a truck to the middle of a San Jose airport runway in the early morning hours with only me and wild rabbits on the fields and waiting three hours to get the right angle of an airplane taking off. It was a photo shoot to be remembered.

Here's looking at you, George . . .

CPSIA information can be obtained
at www.ICGtesting.com
Printed in the USA
LVHW090037211021
701042LV00009B/277/J